Praying with the
PIVOTAL PLAYERS

Amy Welborn

WORD
on FIRE

Word on Fire Catholic Ministries, Park Ridge 60068
© 2016 by Word on Fire Catholic Ministries
Printed in the United States of America
All rights reserved.
Published 2016.
20 19 18 17   2 3 4 5
ISBN: 978-1-943243-14-3

Library of Congress Control Number: 2016947159
Welborn, Amy, 1960-

www.wordonfire.org

Praying with the
PIVOTAL PLAYERS

TABLE *of* CONTENTS

INTRODUCTION

For Christians, holy men and women are more than just pious examples to imitate. They also serve as friends and spiritual guides. Through their own prayers, advice, and spiritual experiences they smooth the path to God and help us find the right way—while ensuring we don't veer in the wrong direction.

You'll meet six such guides in this book, *Praying with the Pivotal Players*, which is an accompaniment to Bishop Robert Barron's groundbreaking film and study program, *CATHOLICISM: The Pivotal Players*. It's not necessary that you watch the accompanying film episodes before using this book, but the film does add color and helpful background to the figures you'll meet here. It will help these devotionals, and the figures behind them, to come alive.

This book contains five short devotional entries for each of the six "pivotal players" featured in Bishop Barron's film series. With thirty total entries, you might choose to read one per day and allow these saints to carry you through an entire month. Or, if you prefer, you can dip in and out of the book, reading more than one entry at a time.

However you choose to use them, we pray that these devotions will introduce you to new spiritual friends, heavenly tour guides who will lead you further down the path of holiness.

—Word on Fire Catholic Ministries

Praying with the
PIVOTAL PLAYERS

DRAWING CLOSER
TO CHRIST

The Lord gave to me, Brother Francis, thus to begin to do penance; for when I was in sin it seemed to me very bitter to see lepers, and the Lord himself led me amongst them and I showed mercy to them. And when I left them, that which had seemed to me bitter was changed for me into sweetness of body and soul. And afterwards I remained a little and I left the world. And the Lord gave me so much faith in churches that I would simply pray and say thus: "We adore thee, Lord Jesus Christ, here and in all thy churches which are in the whole world, and we bless thee, because by thy holy cross thou hast redeemed the world."

So begins Francis' bequest to his brothers, and to us, which was his *Testament*. Dictated not long before his death for the benefit of his growing band of brothers, in it Francis shares advice, reminders, and even some admonitions that sound surprisingly strong, especially to modern ears.

But before all of that, an initial gift: this succinct account of a specific moment that occurred in the midst of that journey to his total conversion to Christ. It makes sense that the autobiographical snippet would begin the bequest, for it was indeed the witness of his life, and specifically the presence of Christ visible in that life, that had drawn the brothers to form family with him in the first place.

From what we know, this meeting occurred somewhere in the midst of Francis' radical Gospel reorientation. Even before this, broken by sorrow for his sins, he had already embraced the life of a penitent. As an expression of this penitential life—one recognized by the Church of the time as a specific call, sometimes even as a part of a formal group of fellow penitents—Francis had separated from his family, embraced deep prayer, practiced mortifications, and given alms. The latter he did with so much enthusiasm that it prompted not only a spiritual but also a legal separation from his family, as his father sought to protect his property from his son's generosity.

Yes, even before this encounter, Francis had heard the call to "rebuild my Church" and this he was doing—literally—down the hill from Assisi in the ruins of San Damiano.

For most of us, this would be plenty. That separation from the familiar for the sake of Christ, the turn from earthly concerns and even family would be enough; it would be further than we could ever imagine traveling from where we sit now, even if we trust that God is leading us.

But Francis was still reaching—more importantly, still *open* to even more. For what else is there to do in this world but to live in a way that gives glory to the God who created you and to Christ who redeemed you? And until you can see the entire world—every bit of it—through the eyes of this infinitely loving Christ, you are not there yet; you are still on the road.

So Francis, lover of beauty, was led among the lepers.

From this and other sources, we can piece together that Francis served in a leprosarium outside of Assisi. All, as he recounts here, while still repulsed by the toll the terrible disease takes on its sufferers.

And in the midst of this, God changed him. What had seemed bitter became sweet, and in showing mercy to those who suffered what he might have called physical ugliness, he experienced mercy for his own spiritual ugliness.

Our own journeys might be characterized at times by questions and uncertainty, by fits and starts, by mysteries. I wonder what God's role is in my spiritual life…and what is my role? How can I know how to discern the ways of God's grace in my life? How can I sense God's will? What signs should I follow? How do I know when to move, when to stand still, when to speak, when to be silent?

This simple, even stark narrative that Francis shares offers a hint. One hint, at least.

It's this: Francis does not sit around. He doesn't wait for a perfect moment to be confirmed in his spiritual intuitions. His life is so deeply prayerful, but see this: anchored by the still place where he meets Christ, Francis *moves*.

Francis knew that to follow Christ means, first of all, to *follow* him. Our feelings are beside the point. Our understanding and analysis can get so much in the way sometimes and become expressions of fear. Our working out of the proper steps and the most appropriate way is wasted time. The first thing the disciple does is what Peter and Andrew did, what Matthew did, what the woman healed of seven demons did: you *move*.

To let Christ in, we simply have to *let him in*, and since Christ is love, we let him in by loving in his name, loving the difficult, loving the unlovable, loving when we are exhausted. We let him in by touching when we would rather draw back, smiling when misery tempts us to turn away, and giving when we think we have nothing left—or when we would really like to just hold on to what we have. But we can do this because it is God, inexhaustible in love, who is at work in us.

No overthinking required. I wonder how I can draw closer to Christ, be more like him and share that joy. It seems pretty complicated at times because life is complicated. Francis shows me that it's not really. It's as simple as setting aside my own desires each day, in great ways and most importantly in small, and just be led amongst my brothers and sisters, and, like him, listen, look, and love whoever is right here in front of me. Now.

Consider: *What opportunities for challenging, sacrificial love have come my way recently?*

Pray: *God of Wisdom, help me discern your movement in my life. Help me see others with the eyes of faith—your eyes.*

NOT AN
IMPOSSIBLE IDEAL

I say to thee: Yes, my son, and as a mother; for in this word and counsel I sum up briefly all the words we said on the way, and if afterwards thou hast need to come to me for advice, thus I advise you: In whatever way it seemeth best to thee to please the Lord God and to follow his footsteps and poverty, so do with the blessing of the Lord God and in my obedience. And if it be necessary for thee on account of thy soul or other consolation and thou wishest, Leo, to come to me, come!

In our memories, the lives of the saints can sometimes collapse into a predetermined narrative. We know how the story ends—with a canonized saint, a holy card, and a statue, and we all know what that is about. In the case of Francis, we also benefit from almost a thousand years of detailed reflection on the life, thought, and legacy of the man.

So as we consider his penitential, deeply sacrificial life, his suffering, all for the sake of Christ, we might think, "Of course he could do all of that. After all, he was *Saint Francis of Assisi!*"

In a way, then, picturing Francis like this gives us both comfort and, if we're honest, an excuse. He could live like this, so, in theory—because he was a person, and we are persons—we can do this, too. But right away, though, given that sheen of eight hundred years of seemingly effortless sanctity, we can also tuck him in the "Amazing Saint!" box and slip him on a shelf to admire, glad he's there, but pretty sure that the depth of his spirituality and commitment must have been in a way *natural* to him...and so probably beyond us.

But Francis? He was a man—a human being. And when you read the accounts, which were admittedly embellished a bit by his admirers through time, an honest read reveals struggle and grief, even after his conversion. We also encounter what should be an obvious truth: we may know how the story has evolved to this point, with hundreds of years of profound and indelible Franciscan influence on the Church and the world—but Francis couldn't see that. He couldn't even see his own tomorrow. He could only listen to the Lord, one day at a time.

The citation above is from a letter Francis wrote to one of his first followers, Brother Leo. It is brief but powerful, in that in it we hear such gentle but strong encouragement. This path? This journey with Christ? Brother Leo, Francis says, you are well on the way.

In order to see how the extraordinary sanctity of Saint Francis might be more possible for you and me than we think, it helps to dig down and try to understand his central focus. We say that Francis embraced a life of following Christ, but what does that mean? Our best source is, of course, Francis himself.

The answer, like any person's actions (even our own), is a bit mysterious, but when we look at Francis' own writings, what we see is that for him, to "live like Christ"—the "poverty" to which he alludes in the letter to Brother Leo—means to embrace total humility.

Christ's great act of poverty was to descend to earth, as Paul relates in Philippians, and empty himself, take the form of a slave, and reject power for the sake of himself.

Physical or economic poverty was certainly a part of that for Francis and his followers, who were prohibited from owning property. Begging ("alms" for Francis included food and other needs, but never money) was intended not as a central, defining activity, but one intended to supply what was still wanting after performing manual labor, and as an expression of humility.

And, it is important to note, nowhere does Francis exhort everyone in the world to abandon all their material goods as a sign of discipleship. That is not to rationalize, but is simply a fact of the case. Most of Francis' exhortations were to his own friars. When it came to the laity, as best we know from his writings, he exhorted them mostly to go to confession and Mass and to live peaceably.

So yes, the core of Francis' own "poverty" was an intense, continual, and challenging abandonment of one's own will.

This is, to Francis, what it means to be "Christlike"—not to be nice, caring, tolerant, or necessarily materially poor. The core of it is, by uniting oneself to Christ, to let Christ—not your own will, goals, desires, ideas, or pride—fill you, guide you, and define you.

As Paul says: "It is not longer I who live but Christ who dwells in me" (Gal 2:20).

It might be interesting to compare Francis' radical message to what voices today tell us about the purpose of our lives—even religious voices. How do they define purpose?

Is my purpose to be my best self? To use my gifts and talents for others? To be "happy?" To live my best life? To be fulfilled?

What I hear from Francis is quite different from all that, and when I follow him to Christ, and listen to him with fresh ears and watch him with my eyes wide open, what I see from him is rather surprising as well. I wonder if the messages about fulfillment, flourishing, and that amazing, exciting life God wants me to have as I become the exciting, awesome person he created me to be have anything to do with the Gospel at all.

I imagine running all this modern talk of fulfillment by Francis. I imagine him sitting on the ground in the ruins of a country chapel, trowel in hand, ragged garments barely keeping out the cold, listening to me prattling on about my best life now and being fulfilled, and being the person God created me to be, and in time—a short time—my words peter out and I just see Francis, and beyond him, that Cross.

Can this radical ideal be attained? Well, it can, clearly. It was Francis' own path, and we read here of him gently encouraging his brothers on that same way. Difficult, challenging, sacrificial, but as possible, especially knowing that on this journey I am not at all alone.

Consider: *What is my understanding of Christian discipleship? How does Francis both challenge me and show me that following Jesus is possible?*

Pray: *Jesus, I trust you when you remind me that your yoke is easy and your burden light. May I take up this yoke today, abandoning my own will, in little ways, for your loving will.*

LIVING IN A
CULTURE OF CORRUPTION

I indeed counsel, warn, and exhort my brothers in the Lord Jesus Christ that when they go through the world they be not litigious nor contend in words, nor judge others; but that they be gentle, peaceful, and modest, meek and humble, speaking honestly to all as is fitting.... Let those brothers to whom the Lord has given the grace of working labor faithfully and devoutly, so that in banishing idleness, the enemy of the soul, they do not extinguish the spirit of holy prayer and devotion, to which all temporal things must be subservient.... The brothers shall appropriate nothing to themselves, neither a house nor place nor anything. And as pilgrims and strangers in this world, serving the Lord in poverty and humility, let them go confidently in quest of alms, nor ought they to be ashamed, because the Lord made himself poor for us in this world. This, my dearest brothers, is the height of the most sublime poverty which has made you heirs and kings of the kingdom of heaven: poor in goods, but exalted in virtue. Let that be your portion, for it leads to the land of the living; cleaving to it unreservedly, my best beloved brothers, for the name of our Lord Jesus Christ, never desire to possess anything else under heaven.

How do we come to know Christ? Not in a featureless, vague vacuum, that is certain. Each of us is invited to discipleship in context, first of our own personalities and personal histories, and

17

then, more broadly, in the context of a culture with its own particular shape, strengths, weaknesses, and sins. So this much is true, but what is also true is that while my ninth- or eighteenth-century counterpart and I might find great bridges of perception and experience to cross, a conversation—if that were possible—would reveal a surprisingly deep commonality.

This is why we still read ancient literature and it can still speak to us. This is why we can see ourselves reflected in centuries-old paintings. And it is why the saints are knowable to us. Augustine lived almost two thousand years ago, but his voice is fresh because we are tempted, just like he was, by shallow entertainment, lust, and the lure of worldly success. Saint Teresa of Avila might have been a celibate, cloistered religious five centuries ago, but that mid-life awakening to the fact that we could be doing much more with our time on earth than we are—well, that is an uncomfortably familiar realization.

Or perhaps, as we understand and connect with our sister across time, it is actually not so uncomfortable, and that realization offers deep comfort—the One who redeemed Teresa, Augustine, and Francis offers redemption and freedom to me as well.

So it is with Francis' world. On the one hand, his culture of courtiers and peasants, of castles and towns, and of countryside peppered with churches, monasteries, and convents, seems quite far from my world. But on the other, the challenges of that culture—compromise and corruption, on both personal and institutional levels—is not so strange to me.

We can discern the elements of that culture that particularly concerned him, which his brothers are being called to step away from and stand in counter-witness to by his own priorities, as he articulated them in his deeds and in his words, such as the passage above, from the 1223 version of the Rule of Francis. What do we see there?

We see a call to a humble, self-effacing life, one not intent on self-defense, self-aggrandizement, or self-promotion. The brothers—"pilgrims" in this world—are to cling to nothing around them, but only Christ.

So this is it: not by activism or a program, but through living in the humility of Christ. This is how Francis invited his brothers to position themselves in the midst of a corrupt, compromised culture. In the midst of compromised ideals and even counter-witness to the Gospel, Francis focused on living out the Gospel himself.

Francis is often described as an "idealist," but what does that mean? In the sense that he sought to live by the highest ideals, the radical humility of Christ, then yes, he was an idealist. In our time, though, "idealist" also has a connotation of one actively working for social change so that a vision of a perfect earthly reality might come to bear. Was Francis an "idealist" intent on "building a better world" or "bringing about the Kingdom of God on earth" in this sense?

It's worth considering that this particular twist on Christian discipleship that prioritizes the shaping of an ideal earthly world is, in fact, a cultural product itself. It's the product of a culture that knows and celebrates material and political "progress" and has the technological means to measure such things. It sees how life was "then," compares it to "now" and announces, "progress!"

Consider, though, that an inhabitant of a small Italian town in the thirteenth century would not have such a perspective. Change was a part of life, of course, as battles were fought, disease struck, storms crushed the harvest. One hoped that his leaders were interested in helping make life better, not worse, although he could never bet on that.

But reform? Yes. However, the "reform" that a pious thirteenth -century Christian would know was essentially of one kind: to purify, to cast out sin and faithlessness, and to cleave more closely to Christ: first, in one's own life, and then, if one had any role to play in an institution, perhaps in that institution. The history of the Church is full of that kind of reform, intentional or accidental.

Francis, according to legend, heard the call from the Cross to "rebuild my Church." What did that mean to him? We think we know. The response, as lived out by the order long after Francis died, probably expresses part of what it means. But in the writings of Francis himself, things are much simpler.

If our lives are not rooted in the radical humility of Christ, the risk of self-interest guiding our actions—even our well-intentioned religious and reforming actions—is high.

Francis allowed himself to be led in this call to "rebuild my Church" not by creating a plan for action focused on a critique of others, but rather by orienting his life towards the humility of Christ, primarily through sacrifice and penance.

And then, as he wrote himself, in the midst of that humble, penitential life, something happened: *The Lord sent me brothers…*

<u>Consider:</u> *What problems in my own circle, my community, church, and culture compel me to passion and action? What frustrations and satisfactions have I experienced in addressing them? What role does pride take in my efforts?*

<u>Pray:</u> *Lord Jesus, people were changed by encountering your mercy, humility, and sacrificial love. Fill me and center me as I navigate a complex world.*

PERFECT JOY

One day in winter, as Saint Francis was going with Brother Leo from Perugia to Saint Mary of the Angels, and was suffering greatly from the cold, he called to Brother Leo, who was walking on before him, and said to him: "Brother Leo, if it were to please God that the Friars Minor should give, in all lands, a great example of holiness and edification, write down, and note carefully, that this would not be perfect joy."

A little further on, Saint Francis called to him a second time: "O Brother Leo, if the Friars Minor were to make the lame to walk, if they should make straight the crooked, chase away demons, give sight to the blind, hearing to the deaf, speech to the dumb, and, what is even a far greater work, if they should raise the dead after four days, write that this would not be perfect joy...."

Now when this manner of discourse had lasted for the space of two miles, Brother Leo wondered much within himself; and, questioning the saint, he said: "Father, I pray thee teach me wherein is perfect joy."

Saint Francis answered: "If, when we shall arrive at Saint Mary of the Angels, all drenched with rain and trembling with cold, all covered with mud and exhausted from hunger...if, urged by cold and hunger, we knock again, calling to the porter and entreating him with many tears to open to us and give us shelter, for the love of God, and if he come out more angry than before, exclaiming, 'These are but importunate rascals, I will deal with them as they

21

deserve'; and, taking a knotted stick, he seize us by the hood, throwing us on the ground, rolling us in the snow, and shall beat and wound us with the knots in the stick—if we bear all these injuries with patience and joy, thinking of the sufferings of our Blessed Lord, which we would share out of love for him, write, O Brother Leo, that here, finally, is perfect joy."

If you asked me about my life's most joyful moments so far, the list would come quickly and easily. I would remember moments of connection and understanding with my children and with friends. I would try to describe dusk on a beach, children darting in and out of the surf. I'd talk about the joy of encountering profoundly creative people and their music, art, and writing, so much of it reaching out to me across centuries. I might mention the cautious, almost fearful joy I've felt in rereading the one or two things I've produced in my vocation as a writer that express true and real things in an almost satisfying way. I'd share with you the deep joy I've experienced in prayer and at Mass.

And then I'd ask you about the joy in your own life, and perhaps your answers would be similar to mine, differing only in time and place and other particulars.

Then we'd both listen to Francis and Brother Leo speaking about joy—perfect joy. I don't know about you, but listening to his vision, now I have to wonder. What is this thing called joy that I thought I knew a bit about?

Once again, Francis challenges and even confounds.

Well, Francis lived in a radical way, and we don't call it radical because he "listened to" or "followed" Jesus in a piecemeal, ultimately very convenient way. It was radical because it was like baptism: full immersion.

In our prayers—the prayers of the psalmist, those inspired by the Gospels and Paul, those we murmur and ponder—we call out to God that yes, we are open to him. We tell God of our yearning for his presence, and the divine grace of beauty, truth, wholeness, and life. Eternally.

The Lord of my life, my savior. *Come, Lord Jesus,* we pray. We welcome sacramental grace, seeking to grow in it and through the encounter with Christ in bread, wine, water, oil, and words uttered in familiar human voices.

Grow how, where, and in what direction? Toward the Son, we pray. We take his name, we pray to be more like him, we willingly trace a sign on our bodies.

A cross.

These other joys? The joys of profoundly connecting to other people, to beauty, truth, and just *life*? Of living in loving service, of living out a vocation? That's joy. But Francis won't let Brother Leo—or us—remain there. It's joy, but it's not *perfect*.

Perfect joy happens in the midst of that full immersion in Christ, which, because we are on earth still and walking in the valley of death and darkness, means that we live in the land where the Cross is still planted.

Not that we shake off those other joyful moments or view them with cynical suspicion because there must be a shadow lurking somewhere. Not that we go seeking out crosses in order to check off that sort of perfect joy.

No. It seems to me that what Francis is challenging me to see is not that those moments aren't joyful, but that when I am trying to love as Christ does, and I suffer because of it, and beautiful sunsets, happy kids, and a stirring symphony are distant memories—well, there is not only joy there too, but indeed perfect joy.

Because it is the Cross, the wounds of which Francis bore on his own body, and, in the midst of that suffering, counted as joy.

This isn't easy. It's very hard.

So there it is. Francis lived out those ancient, enduring yearnings. Our prayers are the same; our souls are made for the Lord and they seek him. Because of sin and its idolatrous invitation to answer these yearnings by means of worldly, dying things, we embrace penance that orients us back to God alone. And so, praying, loving, and embracing the paradox of life-affirming self-denial, we draw closer to Christ and full immersion, and there, because it is Christ we love, when we find him, when we say yes, we find the Cross.

Because it is his, and because love brought us here, yes. It is indeed perfect joy.

Consider: *What have been my life's most joyful moments? How does the "perfect joy" described by Francis challenge or enrich my understanding? How does it help me deal with suffering?*

Pray: *Jesus, may I accept suffering in union with your suffering; and in communion with your perfect love, may I find perfect joy.*

FRANCIS AND CREATION

Praised be You, my Lord, with all Your creatures,

especially Sir Brother Sun,

Who is the day and through whom You give us light.

And he is beautiful and radiant with great splendor;

and bears a likeness of You, Most High One.

Praised be You, my Lord, through Sister Moon and the stars,

in heaven You formed them clear and precious and beautiful.

Praised be You, my Lord, through Brother Wind,

and through the air, cloudy and serene, and every kind of weather,

through whom You give sustenance to Your creatures.

Praised be You, my Lord, through Sister Water,

who is very useful and humble and precious and chaste.

Praised be You, my Lord, through Brother Fire,

through whom You light the night,

and he is beautiful and playful and robust and strong.

Praised be You, my Lord, through our Sister Mother Earth,

who sustains and governs us,

and who produces various fruit with colored flowers and herbs.

Praised be You, my Lord, through those who give pardon for Your love,

and bear infirmity and tribulation.

Blessed are those who endure in peace

for by You, Most High, shall they be crowned.

Praised be You, my Lord, through our Sister Bodily Death,

from whom no one living can escape.

Woe to those who die in mortal sin.

Blessed are those whom death will find in Your most holy will,

for the second death shall do them no harm.

There are certain sayings and prayers attributed to Saint Francis that were not actually penned by him. Most famously—sorry to bear the bad news—the "Prayer of Saint Francis," which begins, "Make me a channel of your peace…" was definitely not his work, and, in fact, can be traced to a World War I-era prayer card popularized by Third Order Franciscans.

But be assured, this "Canticle of the Sun" is indeed from the heart of Francis. It was probably composed in at least two, perhaps three stages.

It is a prayer that is easy to take in a superficial way, and many do, using the *Canticle* along with the stories about Francis and animals and his radically simple lifestyle to paint a portrait in which his respect for God's creation expresses a nature-centered spirituality that is superior to or even stands in opposition to a spiritual life nourished by grace through the teachings, sacraments, and spirituality of Christ's Church.

But reading this prayer carefully, contemplating it in the context of all we know about what Francis actually believed about God, the Church, human nature, and redemption, we see that it makes no sense to claim Francis—who challenged priests to be meticulously careful in their celebration of the Mass and who even, well, *rebuilt* physical church structures— as a standard-bearer for any sort of anti-institutional or nature-centered spirituality.

So, setting aside agendas and expectations and simply listening to Francis sing through his *Canticle*, what do I hear?

In order to hear it with Francis' hopes and intentions in mind, we turn back for a moment to the context in which it was composed.

The bulk of the work was written in 1225, a year before his death, when Francis was undergoing great suffering. It's interesting to note the source of his suffering: his eyes. He was malnourished, suffering from the aftereffects of malaria, and was extremely sensitive to light, even at night, perhaps due to conjunctivitis. It is precisely in this context that Francis composed a hymn praising God for the sun, the moon, and the stars—the objects that caused him such suffering.

As Father Augustine Thompson says in his biography of the saint, Francis had told his brothers of his intention to compose a hymn praising God in the midst of his troubles and joining himself to Christ's Passion.

So now, perhaps, this poem echoes even more profoundly than a simple opportunity to praise God for beautiful things.

And praise it is. That praise, in turn, suggests to me a brief, implicit, but still powerful lesson in "how to pray."

Jesus' disciples asked him that question and he answered it. His answer—the Lord's Prayer—is more than words to take to heart and memorize. They also serve as instructions to me when my own prayer life is leaving me with questions. Much of the time when my prayer feels dry and I wonder where it is going, upon reflection, I discover that what I thought was prayer was really self-referential musing and complaining. When I turn back to Christ and let him teach me, I re-learn the lesson that in prayer, shockingly enough, God comes first. In Jesus' model prayer, acknowledgment and praise of God occupies the first part of the prayer. It's only after that praise that we present our needs to the One we've acknowledged our dependence on.

So, instead of beginning my prayer with "Let me tell you...." I try to retrieve "Thank you...." instead.

So it is with Francis. The *Canticle* is a glorious litany of praise directed to the Creator through his creation. Sometimes, in the popular mind, the prayer is remembered as a praise of those individual elements of creation, but look again. It's God who is praised for the sun, wind, moon, stars, fire, and earth, not those elements praised for their own sake.

The praise Francis sings in the *Canticle* is offered in gratitude for God's power and wisdom, as he experienced it in creation. It's also offered for the way God has fashioned these elements to work in graceful harmony and the gifts that they bring into the lives of us creatures called human beings, in the context, too, of the suffering we bear as a consequence.

As I consider Francis, I keep returning to the word *humility*. The *Canticle* expresses this humility as vividly as does his sacrifice of comfort, security, and personal will and desire. For here Francis situates himself—and the rest of us—quite firmly and properly where we belong: as a creature, part of God's greater plan, gratefully dependent on him and his gifts for our existence.

We are distinct from sun, moon, wind, and other living creatures by the fact that we are made in God's image; that is clear. But Francis, as do all the saints, lives with a keen awareness of his creaturely nature. Francis, intimate with God, sees himself clearly in relation to God and the rest of creation: unique, yet dependent; able to love and live heroically and sacrificially because of God's grace within, yet still just a creature; part of the whole that God brought to birth through his Word, and for whom sister death awaits.

We can get sentimental about Francis and creation, but the *Canticle* is not really sentimental at all, especially when we are aware of Francis' intentions and situation. In the *Canticle*, Francis sings out the praise of the mighty Creator God, who has fashioned an intricate world of power, beauty, and grace of which we are part.

Because of our created nature, we share in this beauty. We also share in the suffering of creation, which is ennobled and sanctified by the suffering of Christ, who shares our creaturely nature.

So, humbly accepting our created state, we know that our bodies are like the bodies of the trees, the fish, and the stones that wear down under our feet. Accepting and aware, and humbly joined to Christ's passion, we can welcome sister death because this is who we are. And we can do so unafraid, trusting that bodily death is not our end because Christ is also who we are.

Consider: *What is my sense of myself as part of God's creation? How can I, like Francis, join the sufferings and limitations I bear as a creature to the sufferings of Christ, and praise God through it?*

Pray: *Creator God, I thank and praise you for my life and for all of creation. In humility, I praise you for all you have made, even that which brings me suffering, for in that I am joined to Christ.*

ST. CATHERINE *of* SIENA

SELF-KNOWLEDGE

For I told you in the beginning that one comes to knowledge of the truth through self-knowledge. But self-knowledge alone is not enough: it must be seasoned by and joined with knowledge of me within you. This is how you found humility and contempt for yourself along with the fire of my charity, and so came to love and affection for your neighbors and gave them the service of your teaching and your holy and honorable living.

By any standard of any era—thirteenth- or twenty-first—Catherine of Siena was a remarkable woman. In fact, the twenty-first century finds much to praise her for, and in terms that it finds comfortable and familiar. She was successful and achieved a great deal. She enjoyed widespread fame and popularity. She was respected and had great influence. She thought and even lived outside the box in ways quite unlike other people, especially women of her time. She used the gifts and talents God gave her in heroic service to others.

Catherine had a lot to be proud of. She must have felt very good about herself!

But wait. What is this?

In the passage above, from Catherine's *Dialogue*, she relays her experience of God's word to her, recounting how she had found "humility" and "contempt" for herself.

Is this a good thing? *Contempt* for oneself? That sounds a lot like having a negative self-image, and we all know how important it is to avoid that.

Perhaps translating Catherine for my own time is not as simple as I thought. Perhaps she, like Francis—and every other Catholic saint—confounds my sense of what life is about, makes me suspect that I am formed more strongly by modernity than I thought, and plants me right in the middle of that paradox that comes directly from Christ himself:

> *He who would save his life must lose it. The last*
> *shall be first.*

The paradox, as it reaches me through Catherine's experience, is that of a fruitful, joyous, peaceful life built on a foundation of "contempt" for oneself. What does this mean?

It begins with the reality, so essential to Catherine, of truth. The fundamental truth, of course, is not an idea, but God. The only real way to *be* is in relationship to the Truth that created us so that we can, indeed, know him. When we know who God is, we know who we are. When we know who we are—beloved, weak, tempted creatures made in God's image, in need of redemption lest we be lost—we can reach out to the only One who can, indeed, save us. And here rests the paradox: as we embrace Truth, we humbly accept our emptiness and dependence on God, and then we can finally be filled—to overflowing, even.

> *Here is the way, if you would come to perfect knowl-*
> *edge and enjoyment of me, eternal Life. Never leave*
> *the knowledge of yourself. Then, put down as you*
> *are in the valley of humility, you will know me in*
> *yourself, and from this knowledge you will draw all*
> *that you need.*

So this denial of self, humility, and what Catherine calls "contempt" —these are not at all about hatred of one's self as God's creation (which would be blasphemous), a disparagement of one's own existence or of human nature and qualities.

It is simply the only truthful way to live in the real world, the only honest way to walk on this earth permeated by the transcendent that brought it forth and sustains it still—to understand my place: a weak creature graced, if I say yes, with the chance to be filled to overflowing with infinite Love.

This helps us understand Catherine's life and activity. We speak of "success" and "achievement," but Catherine uses other language. She speaks of understanding her own smallness and weakness, accepting it, and only then being radically open to God's grace at work in her. She would not claim credit, as we would give it, for her "abilities": her boldness, courage and self-assurance, her willingness to stand out, her defiance of convention, her leadership, her spiritual insights.

The saints are a varied lot. They are extroverts, introverts, rich, poor, young, old, artists, queens, beggars, scholars, and doorkeepers. But all of them, Catherine included, embody authentic humility. Their sense of a life well-lived challenges mine. Success? Achievement? Opportunity? Talents? I sometimes wonder how to navigate all of those values, especially as a disciple of Jesus. I'm here on earth right now. I'm willing and able. What am I supposed to do and how am I supposed to figure it out? In Catherine, I get a glimpse of another landscape, one not that far away after all, one peopled by those who know the truth of who they are, how precious and yet how small; who know their own weaknesses; and who know that God's infinite strength is as close as their own *fiat*.

> *By this gentle glorious light the soul sees and*
> *rightly despises her own weakness; and by so*
> *making a fool of herself she gains mastery of*

the world, treading it underfoot with her love,
scorning it as worthless.

Consider: *When I think about "knowing myself," what is that I
think of? How does Catherine balance an understanding of herself as
a beloved child of God with honesty about her own weaknesses? How
can I?*

Pray: *Creator God, you loved me into existence. Yet I am so small
and weak. I pray for a heart open to be filled with your grace, strength,
love, and wisdom.*

ST. CATHERINE *of* SIENA

HOLY DESIRE

O eternal, infinite Good! O mad lover! And you have need of your creature? It seems so to me, for you act as if you could not live without her, in spite of the fact that you are Life itself, and everything has life from you and nothing can have life without you. Why then are you so mad? Because you have fallen in love with what you have made! You are pleased and delighted over her within yourself, as if you were drunk with desire for her salvation. She runs away from you and you go looking for her. She strays and you draw closer to her. You clothed yourself in our humanity, and nearer than that you could not have come.

From the beginning of our lives on earth, we are buffeted by and confused by desire. Born helpless, we first know only need, but then, along with growing awareness, we discover longing and desire, and then, in quick succession, frustration and loss. Sitting here today, we can perhaps even describe the course of our lives in terms of desire. "This isn't what I wanted." "I've achieved most of what I wanted to." "I should have been more careful of what I wished for...I didn't know what would happen when I got it." "What do I want to do with the rest of my life? Let me tell you...."

The price of desire—frustration, disappointment, exploitation—and its place in human experience means that it also has a place in spirituality. Some religious traditions—most famously, Buddhism—address desire by denigrating its role in human life, defining it as a problem (all suffering, the Buddha taught, comes from desire), and even teaching that the key to human fulfillment is the extinction of desire.

Christianity doesn't teach this.

This surprises people sometimes because of the importance of self-denial in the Christian tradition, beginning with Jesus himself, who spoke to his disciples about denying oneself and carrying crosses, and then lived that out. Surely this emphasis is really about simply suppressing desire and passionate connection?

No. Despite the profound value of asceticism in Christian tradition, Christianity does not, in fact, disparage desire itself. As a matter of fact, longing runs through Christian spirituality, unapologetic, even passionate longing, expressed on both sides of the divine-human dynamic. It's all over what God has revealed to us about his love for his beloved lost creatures in Scripture; it pulsates through Christian spiritual experience and expression; and few embody this reality more powerfully than Catherine of Siena herself.

In the passage above, Catherine addresses God; and "she" refers, of course, to Catherine. A spirituality in which God is told he is a "mad lover" and "drunk with desire" and "in love" is not one of careful reserve, of disengagement, or of a careful, restrictive, effete understanding of "love."

So how do desire and self-denial coexist? How is this not simply incoherent?

Well, elsewhere in the *Dialogue*, Catherine writes, perhaps influenced by Saint Augustine, whose writings we know she was familiar with, of human beings' misplaced and misdirected desires. We are made by God to be his own, yearning for unconditional, faithful love; rock-solid, trustworthy truth;

changeless beauty; and the everlasting life of our Father, our source. Much of our unhappiness, sin, and missteps are the consequence of making idols of earthly things, looking to the finite to satisfy the longing for the only thing can complete us—the infinite gifts of our Creator.

And so, Catherine challenges us to ask ourselves, quite simply, why settle? Consider the truth—and Catherine is all about the truth—of your existence. You are here on earth, and why? Because God loves you and wants you to be here. Why did Jesus come to earth? Because God loves you and wants to rescue you from sin, wants you to live forever. This is the truth of life, this is the truth of your life and mine, that Love put us here— greater love than we can even imagine, such love that requires the most ecstatic language to even come close to describing.

We can and certainly must love the people and created things of our world, but, as Augustine wrote many times, in ways proper to their nature, not making the peace of our souls dependent on our relationship to them. God alone is worthy of that kind of love, indeed, that passion. So the denial of the self and of earthly things is really the proper ordering and directing of our desires.

So, in Catherine we see serious, even what we might call extreme, spiritual discipline and self-denial, but then, paradoxically to the world, we turn and hear deep passion and witness tremendous fruitfulness. And yes, it's passion we encounter in Catherine. Passion for the God who is passionate for her, the fruit of which is a passion for souls.

> *Then you are roused with eager longing, thirsty to follow the way of Truth that leads to the fountain of living water. Your thirst for my honor and for your own and your neighbors' salvation makes you long for the way, for without the way you could never reach what you thirst for. So walk on, carrying your*

heart like a vessel emptied of every desire and every disordered earthly love. But no sooner is your vessel emptied than it is filled. For nothing can remain empty. If it is not full of something material, it will fill up with air. Just so, the heart is a vessel that cannot remain empty. As soon as you have emptied it of all those transitory things you loved inordinately, it is filled with air—that is, with gentle, heavenly, divine love that brings you to the water of grace. And once you have arrived there you pass through the gate, Christ crucified, to enjoy that living water— for now, you find yourself in me, the sea of peace.

I consider my own life, prayerfully. Catherine challenges me to consider my own relationship with the people and things of the world and to honesty judge if I might be making idols of them. Fear sometimes can enter as we weigh the role of these desires in our lives and picture what it might mean to live differently. We might be afraid that looking at desire in a spiritual way might cut us off from the world or lessen our connections with others. Catherine shows me vividly—and, even more importantly, joyfully—that the fruit of being passionately open to God's desire for us and recognizing that my deepest desire is for him, this is nothing to be afraid of.

Consider: *What are my deepest desires? What do I believe will bring me happiness on a daily and a long-term basis? What deeper desires for the permanence that God promises are hidden in my worldly desires?*

Pray: *Lord, you are the one who answers my deepest longings. In setting aside earthly objects, may I approach a deeper communion with you and others.*

BLOOD

At the end of his life, stripped naked, scourged at the pillar, parched with thirst, he was so poor on the wood of the cross that neither the earth nor the wood could give him a place to lay his head. He had nowhere to rest it except on his own shoulder. And drunk as he was with love, he made a bath for you of his blood when this Lamb's body was broken open and bled from every part.... He was sold to ransom you with his blood. By choosing death for himself he gave you life.

Blood. Some of us are wary of the sight or even repulsed by it, but in Catherine's landscape, there is no turning away. The biological truth that blood is life and the transcendent truth that the blood of Christ is eternal life are deeply embedded in her spirituality. We see it in the *Dialogue*, in passages like the one above, and even in her correspondence.

For in her letters, Catherine usually begins by immediately setting the context of the message that is about to come:

> *Catherine, servant and slave of the servants of Jesus Christ, writes to you in his precious blood...*

The salutation is followed by a brief statement of her purpose, which, by virtue of Catherine's initial positioning of her words in the context of the life-giving blood of Jesus, bear special weight and authority:

> *in his precious blood... desiring to see you a true servant...desiring to see you obedient daughters... desiring to see you burning and consumed in his blazing love...desiring to see you clothed in true and perfect humility...*

In both the *Dialogue* and her letters, Catherine takes this fundamental truth about salvation—that it comes to us through the death, that is, the blood of Christ—and works with it in vivid, startling ways. She meets the challenges of describing the agonies and ecstasies of the spiritual life with rich, even wild metaphors, and the redemptive blood of Christ plays its part here. For as she describes this life of a disciple, we meet Christ's friends, followers, sheep, and lovers as those drunk on his blood, inebriated. They are washed in the blood and they even drown in it:

> *This is how these beloved children and faithful servants of mine follow the teaching and example of my Truth... Indeed, they go into battle filled and inebriated with the blood of Christ crucified. My charity sets this blood before you in the hostel of the mystic body of holy Church to give courage...*

> *Indeed they will pass through the narrow gate drunk, as it were, with the blood of the spotless Lamb, dressed in charity for their neighbors, and bathed in the blood of Christ crucified, and they will find themselves in me, the sea of peace, lifted above imperfection and emptiness into perfection and filled with every good.*

We drink the blood, served to us, as Catherine's vision presents it, by God himself in the hostel, or inn, of the Church. We are not just strengthened by this drink: the blood of Christ renders us drunk in him, drunk with love. What does this even mean? How can drunkenness, even on what Christ gives us, be a good thing?

Perhaps it is that when filled with the blood of Christ we are satiated, as the one who desires drink above all glows with contented, even joyful satisfaction when he has his fill. Although each person's response to alcohol is different, Catherine's usage certainly implies a picture of the happy drunk, one who has taken in what he has desired to the point of carefree, almost fearless joy.

But more than that—although this certainly touches on a dark edge of alcohol—if a person is inebriated, this implies a lack of control. In our earthly, physical life, this is certainly an unfortunate thing, but in Catherine's spirituality, the imagery takes this loss of control and turns into a vision of being filled with Christ, satiated to the point that it is his power that has taken over our will and moves us. We are in his thrall, the thrall of divine love.

In a letter to her closest spiritual advisor, Raymond of Capua, written the year of her death, Catherine alludes to the blood in a different way:

> *I beg you, dearest Father, to pray earnestly that you and I together may drown ourselves in the blood of the humble Lamb. This will make us strong and faithful.*

We are bathed, washed, and drowned in the blood of Christ at baptism. As time goes on, we grow in faith and love, and we understand who we are—so important to Catherine—more clearly. This act of drowning, remember, is not a negative to Catherine. She echoes Paul, who in Romans describes baptism as the act of dying and rising with Christ (and remember that in the early Church, adults were baptized nude in a tomb-shaped font in the earth, being born again, dying, and rising all at once.) Catherine understands that self-knowledge of our true selves only comes in Christ, and not simply knowing about Christ or admiring his sayings, but in the shockingly loving, bloody sacrifice on the Cross.

What do we find out? We see—in the blood—our true value, as beloved and redeemed. Eyes opened, and filled to the point of inebriation with this loving gaze of Christ, we then look at others in perhaps a different way. Christ's blood was shed not just for me, but for everyone I see and encounter during the course of a day, every struggling, tempted, searching child of God. Catherine's vision invites me to consider how much I really let Christ into my life, how much I give over to him, how fully I have allowed the grace of baptism to really cleanse me, free me, and fill me, how much I am resisting, and how much I have allowed myself to consume and be consumed.

Consider: *How do I think of my life in relationship to God, who created me, loves me, and redeems me? Do I hold back from God or is he truly my life's blood?*

Pray: *Loving Jesus, in your death, I find life.*

ST. CATHERINE *of* SIENA

THE BRIDGE

I showed you the bridge as well. And I showed you the three ordinary stairs that are set up in the soul's three powers, and how no one can have the life of grace without climbing all three stairs, without gathering all three powers in my name. Then I revealed to you how these stairs were in a special way a figure of the three spiritual stages, symbolized in the body of my only begotten Son. I told you that he had made a stairway of his body, and showed it to you in his nailed feet, in his open side, and in his mouth where the soul tastes peace and calm.

I showed you the imperfection of slavish fear and the imperfection of love that loves me for the delight it feels. And I showed you the perfection of the third stage, of those who have attained peace at his mouth. These have run with eager longing across the bridge of Christ crucified. They have climbed the three ordinary stairs, have gathered their souls' three powers and all their works in my name...

Christ as a bridge is one of the best-known images of Catherine's visions and writing. It is also, the more you read about it, one of the more complex and possibly confusing, for it suggests far more than just a simple span between heaven and earth. Catherine returns to the image over and over again through the *Dialogue*, building and expanding upon it so that it expresses ever more densely the nature of and stages in the spiritual journey. It's worth a bit of unpacking.

43

To visualize the bridge, it's helpful to remember that in Catherine's time, a bridge could be more than a stretch of wood or stone. It could be an actual neighborhood. Particularly in a large town or city, a bridge might be lined with shops or tightly packed homes or even a chapel. Not an inch would be wasted. A bridge, especially those in the midst of cities that were constructed mainly for pedestrian use rather than that of wheeled vehicles, would also have steps on either side of the middle rise.

Catherine's bridge is the crucified body of Christ. It is the path by which God has given his beloved, weak creatures a way back home to him. Christ's body breaches the gap between heaven and earth, "joining the most high with the most lowly," and it also lifts those on the journey safely above the raging, threatening river of worldly temptation and sin. Like the medieval bridge, this bridge of Christ's body has walls and a roof (of mercy) to protect the travelers, and a hostelry, or inn, where the travelers are "served the bread of life and the blood, lest the journeying pilgrims, my creatures, grow weary and faint on the way."

Christ was the living bridge, uniting earth and heaven, human and divine, when he was on earth; and now, the Church and its teachings are the remaining "bridgeway" to salvation and truth. As we read above, Catherine then equates the steps of this bridge with spiritual stages, which in turn correspond to elements of Christ's body.

In the early stages of the journey, the believer encounters the nailed feet of Christ. Those at this stage, Catherine says, believe and have a sort of faith, but are motivated by fear of God's punishment, what she calls a "slavish fear."

Moving on, they encounter the side of Christ, opened by the spear, and hence his heart. This type of faith has moved beyond a fear of punishment, yes, but the motivation is still imperfect. She describes it as a "mercenary" attachment and an expression of a "spiritual sensuality." That is, the believer has faith because it evokes happiness and other positive feelings. Faith here rests on the experience of consolations. It is imperfect still, "for they serve me for their own profit or for the delight and pleasure they find in me."

Both of these previous steps are indeed steps on the journey of faith, so they are not false, lies, or deceptions. But they are not the fullest, deepest possible relationship with God. That is experienced when the pilgrim arrives at the mouth of Christ, and rests in him with a filial love—the trusting, accepting love of a child for a parent. Our own interests and concerns are set aside, and we can allow ourselves to be filled with the love of God for his own sake. We know who God is; we know who we are; we now live in what is real, not in fantasies built out of pride, fantasies of independence and power that rest on the false gods of earthly pleasure.

Many of us, when confused or at a loss, find it helpful to make lists and draw charts. I know I do. Books are written, plans proposed to help businesses get back on track by virtue of clarifying flowcharts. Our spiritual pain, too, becomes the subject of systems, plans, and diagrams. Catherine's bridge can't be reduced in that way. I don't know how you would even begin to draw it, not just because it would be a challenge just to depict the crucified Christ as a bridge spanning both worldly rivers and heaven and earth, but also because into it she pours the whole of human experience, and you can't draw that.

The particular details of the bridge draw our interest. We look for ourselves in the three different groups—mindful that Catherine pointed out that one person could embody all three "stages," even at the same time. We can reflect on the reality of Christ as our link between heaven and earth, looking to him when we find either one difficult to understand or cope with.

Tempted by sin, we can visualize the temptation as that deadly river, remember that we have the bridge of Christ to keep us safe, and remain there.

But besides all of that, the bare fact of the complexity and density of Catherine's image gives food for thought and prayer. In intense communion with God, this young woman entered into a profound understanding of the realities of human life.

I want life to be simple. I want other people to be more transparent. I wish my own journey, my choices, and the trajectory of my life, past, present, and future, were clearer to me. I have a home life, a work life, complicated relationships, memories, the confusing events of the greater world, the mystery of eternal life, the constant invitation of Christ to go deeper and what I know that will cost me. Envisioning my journey as a straight path doesn't help. But envisioning myself on the bridge, in the company of crowds of other complicated, inconsistent pilgrims, protected by the Word made flesh—that does.

Consider: *What are my motivations in my spiritual life? What brings me to God's presence? What elements of Catherine's bridge are most striking or helpful to me?*

Pray: *Lord Jesus, you are the bridge between heaven and hearth. You are the way to mercy, peace, and joy. Give me shelter and show me the way to safety.*

ST. CATHERINE *of* SIENA

CHARITY

Now this is how the soul acts who has in truth reached the third stair. This is the sign that she has reached it: Her selfish will died when she tasted my loving charity, and this is why she found her spiritual peace and quiet in the mouth.... She has let go and drowned her own will, and when that will is dead there is peace and quiet. She brings forth virtue for her neighbors without pain. Not that this is in itself painless, but the dead will feels no pain because it endures pain willingly for my name's sake.

Catherine was beloved and esteemed during her lifetime for the manner in which she lived out her devotion to Christ. She was a mystic—contemplative, perceptive, open, and intense in her communion with the Lord, as well as tirelessly active: truthful, passionate, courageous, and compassionate. Coursing underneath and within all of these aspects of her character, energizing them all, was that essential virtue of *caritas*, love.

But as Catherine would say herself, love has a source. It is not something that we achieve or accomplish or attain thanks to our own power. We love, as the first letter of John explains, because God has loved us first, breathing us into existence, redeeming us through the blood of Christ. We are able to love because of the communion we have with God through the lovingly shed blood of Christ, and for no other reason. The closer in communion we are with him, the more we are able to love.

So in the excerpt above from the *Dialogue*, Catherine shares what she has come to understand through her deep prayer, building on the image of the bridge: the one who has moved beyond motivations of slavish fear or mercenary need to feel consolation from serving God, this one has now reached the mouth of Christ. There she rests in love, she is filled with it, and she can love all those around her without worrying about the cost or how it makes her feel. In union with Love, she loves.

Sometimes in considering Catherine, we focus on the remarkable mysticism and forget the fruit. Yes, Catherine began her intense spiritual life by spending a few years as a cloistered contemplative in her own home, but in time, she emerged, empowered to live out the spiritual and corporal works of mercy joyfully and at great cost. All of her activity—the activism focused on the papacy, the Papal States, and the other Italian city-states; the preaching; the letter-writing and spiritual guidance; and, most vividly, the tending to the sick and impoverished—all of it is rooted in love, and not just any love, but the sacrificial, disinterested love of Jesus Christ.

It seems extraordinary, as does much of Catherine's life. But it would be ironic if this young woman's extraordinary witness to love discouraged us, or if we held her up as an example too far beyond us to even attempt to emulate. Catherine herself poured out the insights she had gained through prayer and mysticism in her letters and in the *Dialogue*, not to set herself up as an icon, but as a means of revealing the truth about God, a truth for everyone: God is as close as your open heart, a heart that was created out of love, to be loved, and to love:

> *Thus have I given you reason—necessity, in fact—to practice mutual charity. For I could well have supplied each of you with all your needs, both spiritual and material. But I wanted to make you dependent on one another so that each of you would be my*

minister, dispensing the graces and gifts you have
received from me. So whether you will it or not,
you cannot escape the exercise of charity! Yet, unless
you do it for love of me, it is worth nothing to you
in the realm of grace.

So you see, I have made you my ministers, setting
you in different positions and in different ranks to
exercise the virtue of charity. For there are many
rooms in my house. All I want is love. In loving me
you will realize love for your neighbors, and if you
love your neighbors you have kept the law. If you are
bound by this love you will do everything you can to
be of service wherever you are.

Love is defined so many different ways through history and
even in our own culture. Discerning what authentic love is
and how to live it can be a continual challenge for us. In our
prayer, we often focus on just this question. What does it
mean to love this difficult family member? Where is the love
that I yearn for? What is acting in a loving way supposed to
feel like? I am called to love all people; how do I do that? As
a disciple of Jesus, love is supposed to define my life and my
actions. Does it, really?

For the Christian, the answer begins in Jesus. If God is love,
the way to discern how to love, and if what I am living out is
actually love or something else, is to look to God—revelation
in Scripture and tradition, and the Word of God, Jesus Christ.

Mercifully, I also have the lives of the saints, held up to me
by the Church, because these men and women embody the
Gospel and the virtues in remarkable ways. Look to Jesus, and
look to his beloved friend, Catherine:

She runs briskly along the way of the teaching
of Christ crucified.... She loves me for myself,

because I am supreme Goodness and deserve to be loved, and she loves herself and her neighbors because of me, to offer glory and praise to my name. And therefore she is patient and strong in suffering, and persevering.

Consider: *What is my understanding of love? How does Catherine's experience of God's love challenge me? How does it comfort me? Where does the love of God call me to go from here, today?*

Pray: *Heavenly Father, you are love. I love you and I praise you. Fill me with your love so that I might love with courage.*

MICHELANGELO

INCARNATION AND CREATIVITY

I honor all matter besides, and venerate it. Through it, filled, as it were, with a divine power and grace, my salvation has come to me. Was not the thrice happy and thrice blessed wood of the Cross matter? Was not the sacred and holy mountain of Calvary matter? What of the life-giving rock, the Holy Sepulchre, the source of our resurrection: was it not matter? Is not the most holy book of the Gospels matter? Is not the blessed table matter which gives us the Bread of Life? Are not the gold and silver matter, out of which crosses and altar-plate and chalices are made? And before all these things, is not the body and blood of our Lord matter? Either do away with the veneration and worship due to all these things, or submit to the tradition of the Church in the worship of images, honoring God and his friends, and following in this the grace of the Holy Spirit. Do not despise matter, for it is not despicable. Nothing is [despicable] which God has made.

-Saint John Damascene on the material world

Jesus Christ, the "image of the invisible God," entered the world to redeem it, to gather it to himself. This incarnation— the invisible God embodied in flesh—has implications not just for us individually as we relate to God, but to the entirety of human life and to the whole of creation as well.

For we are not pure spirit, and this reconciling presence of Christ reaches us through the entirety of our creaturehood:

51

soul, spirit, intellect, reason, and even the matter out of which we are composed and upon which we live our earthly days: this earth.

The implications of this truth—that creation itself and what we fashion out of it can be occasions through which God reveals himself—have been controversial throughout Christian history. Let us look especially to the seventh century, when this challenge was met by the great theologian Saint John Damascene. His words above reminded his listeners (and us) that we are matter, that matter is created by God and by no means spurned by him, and that it's through matter that God reaches out to us.

What John articulated and what our faith embraces is really the implication of the incarnation. Christ was encountered through the touch of his hands, the sounds of his voice, the bread and wine he made into himself; and he has not left us orphaned. Still with us, he even now meets us through water, oil, bread, wine, and the human voice.

The incarnational, sacramental nature of life is more surely and trustworthily embodied in the Body of Christ, through its sacraments and sacramentals. But outside of specifically religious practice, beauty dwells, flourishes, grows, is shaped, and reveals. We perceive this beauty through our senses. We come to know God's power, reason, creativity, and love through his creation, and we grow closer to him, and our spirits soar and flourish, as we embrace and engage the glimmer of creativity he has given to us, men and women, as Genesis reveals, made in God's image.

We look to Michelangelo Buonarroti as one who embodies all of this in a spectacular, notable, and noble way. Obsessed with the beauty of God's creation, particularly the miracle of the human body, he threw himself into a lifelong partnership with God to use his own brilliant gifts to create something new and revelatory.

We don't look to him as "pivotal" because he was saint, but because his art represents, as Bishop Barron says, "the full flowering of the Catholic artistic tradition," brilliantly showing how art—beauty—can "be a route of access to God and a means of evangelization."

But there is a paradox here, woven even into the Catholic embrace of beauty and the power of human artistic endeavor. It is that in all of this, the beauty and harmony of God's creation—and in what we create by working with God's gifts—we find and hear hints of the Creator, yet in the end, they still all fall short.

We are not animists or deep Romantics who worship nature or human endeavors. We are brought into deeper communion with each other, with the best part of ourselves, and with the divine by the light creation sheds, and we are grateful for natural beauty and the fruit of human creativity. But we also know that God is, hard as it is to imagine, even more beautiful, more glorious, more harmonious, profound, and perfect than any of it.

No one knows this better than the artist himself, who lives and works with a constant level of low-grade frustration because whatever he can fashion, write, or compose can never perfectly express the depth, breadth, beauty, and truth of the image in his mind. A writer once declared that no one ever "finishes" writing a book—you just give up. Michelangelo himself expressed this frustration in a poem he wrote late in his life:

> In such slavery, and with so much boredom,
> and with false conceptions and great peril
> to my soul, to be here sculpting divine things.

Scholars believe that during the time he wrote this poem, out of frustration with his work, Michelangelo actually smashed part of a *pietà* he was sculpting for his own tomb. So even this is an apt image for our relationship to God, and also a caution: our words, thoughts, concepts, and images point to the Divine, but always fall short of the majesty of God, and, in the face of this reality, we are grateful for the *imago Dei* that we bear, which permits us to even approach the light and capture a glimmer of it. Yet we are also humble, because only God is God.

All of us live, gratefully, in this world of created matter, through which God continuously reminds us, if we are paying attention, of his majesty, power, harmony, and paradoxical beauty in simplicity. We see, we take note, we pray, we connect.

And while none of us are Michelangelo, each of us, in ways great and small throughout the day, partner with God, using the creative spark within to fashion new things that can, if properly situated and directed, be a small space in which that same beauty, truth, and harmony are reflected: a meal, a garden, a neat row of stitches on a garment, a smoothly-running machine or section of computer code, a school project, a story told to a sleepy child, a joke shared to ease an awkward moment, a comforting note.

A child hums as she stacks her blocks. It may sound tuneless and random, her construction may be unbalanced and soon tumble to the floor, but the girl's urge to create is real and persistent. Like Michelangelo's, it stirs deep within, in a place deeper than she can articulate, but one as close to her as the One who mysteriously breathed life into her, in his own creative image.

<u>Consider:</u> *What are the various ways I engage my own creativity during the day? What beauty speaks to me of God's own harmony, beauty, and glory?*

<u>Pray:</u> *Creator God, you are life, truth, and beauty. May I be more nurturing of my own and others' creativity and more attentive to beauty, which brings glory to you.*

MICHELANGELO

THE LIFE OF
AN ARTIST

If you should find that you have been more heavily dealt with than other folk, do all you can to avoid paying, and let them rather take everything you possess: let me know what happens. But if you find that others have received exactly the same treatment, be patient and trust in God.... Look to your life and health, and if you cannot share the honors of the land like other citizens, be content that you have bread to eat; and live well with Christ, and poorly, as I do here. I live in a miserable fashion, caring neither for life nor for honors, and I suffer excessive hardships, assailed by a thousand anxieties. It is now about fifteen years since I had an hour's repose, and all that I have ever done has been to help you: and you have never recognized this nor believed it. God pardon us all! I am ready to go on doing as I have done as long as I live, provided I am able.

-Letter from Michelangelo to his father

We know Michelangelo by his great works—the *David*, the *Pietà*, the Sistine Chapel ceiling, and *Last Judgment*. The core of his genius, like any genius, is an awe-inspiring mystery. To know that the *Pietà* was completed when he was just twenty-five years old is indeed a mystery, and quite humbling.

But Michelangelo, the genius, was not a god. He was a man with limits, both external and internal. He was man with conflicts and strengths and weaknesses. He was a man with family that pulled on him, friends who disappointed and delighted him, associates and employers who enraged him. He was a man who faced death, wondering about and even being concerned for his salvation.

We know much about the life of Michelangelo, not only from contemporary accounts and biographies written soon after his death, but also from his own letters and poems. He left scores of both, and from them we can learn much about the artistic genius.

We cannot, however, learn much about his creative process, which is disappointing to some. Even his poetry rarely touches directly on the themes of creativity or art, centering mostly on reflections about his friends and associates, and, in the latter part of his life, spiritual themes, sometimes in agonizing ways.

However, while his letters tell us little about the internal process of artistic creation, they tell us a great deal about the external forces and elements of his life, in fascinating and even amusing ways. And definitely ways that all of us, genius or not, can relate to. For example:

> *Enough; it is only what I deserve for having believed in other people for thirty years and for having placed myself freely at their service: painting, sculpture, hard work, and too much faith have ruined me, and everything goes from bad to worse. How much better it would have been if in my early days I had been set to make sulfur matches, for then I should not have all this anxiety!*

Michelangelo lived an incessantly busy, very long life—he died at the age of 89. He never married, but supported his family—father, siblings, and their families—for his entire life. He loaned money, gave money outright as charity, invested in businesses, provided dowries for female relatives who were marrying or entering the convent. We can discern that sometimes this lifelong support was appreciated, but at times, at least from the artist's perspective, it was not, at least not to his satisfaction.

His letters to family members, patrons both clerical and lay, and other artists and business associates are detailed, emotional, direct, and often aggravated. He discusses his contractual issues with Pope Julius II, as well as some of the other thirteen popes who reigned during his lifetime. He lamented his kidney stones. He wondered what had become of his investments. He detailed the work and money he had put into his art and preparation for his work (supervising the cutting of stone, for example) without fair compensation from his patrons. He wrote of his housing and workshop problems, issues with servants and assistants, and he regularly issued directives on almsgiving.

The family letters are to his father, brother, and nephew, and express a great deal of aggravation with everything from money issues, questions of marriage ("as for beauty, as you are not yourself the most handsome youth in Florence, it skills not for you to trouble overmuch about it…"), his puzzlement at the gifts his nephew keeps sending him, and his extreme annoyance at his nephew's terrible handwriting: "As I was quite unable to decipher your last letter, I put it into the fire…"

Michelangelo was not a saint. His personality, work process, and personal life are not models for anyone else—despite people writing management and self-help books like *The Michelangelo Method* with that goal in mind. His apparent choice to sacrifice personal relationships for the sake of art is not the point. But the prayerful, conscious disciple of Jesus can take something away from contemplating the artist's life through the lens of his letters and poetry.

We can think, here I am, living my life. This is it, right now. I have gifts, I have a yearning to use them in service, to contribute something good, beautiful, and helpful. I believe that's part of what discipleship is all about.

But the constraints!

Shall we list them? Family responsibilities. Health issues. The need to simply make a living right now, in this place. Others not fulfilling their own part of the bargain. In short, a very complicated, busy life, pulled this way and that.

If only... I wish... then I could...

This is not about saying, "Look at what Michelangelo overcame! You can do it!"

Not at all. It is simply about recognizing the temptation to wait for the perfect moment to live life and to serve in the way we discern the Spirit is nudging us. We can't wait for situations to be straightened out, for the right moment, for everyone to be getting along, for every single perceived obstacle to be cleared away.

Michelangelo's letters show that there is no such thing as the perfect, peaceful, harmonious moment waiting for my activity. Life offers constant crosses and trials, human beings are who they are, my life is constrained, and I am a creature, sorely limited by internal and external factors.

Well, welcome to the human race. This is it. Right now, so much is happening: brothers and sisters are in need, my gifts are being called upon, my loving service is being invited. There is no perfect moment to wait for. There is only this moment, here, where I live now.

Consider: *The limitations and constraints I experience are real. How can I discern how to best serve the Lord and his people within those limitations?*

Pray: *Lord, you are here with me right now, in this moment. Enlighten me and strengthen me to do your will and love and serve as you would have me do today.*

MICHELANGELO

DAVID

For in it may be seen most beautiful contours of legs, with attachments of limbs and slender outlines of flanks that are divine; nor has there ever been seen a pose so easy, or any grace to equal that in this work, or feet, hands, and head so well in accord, one member with another, in harmony, design, and excellence of artistry. And, of a truth, whoever has seen this work need not trouble to see any other work executed in sculpture, either in our own or in other times, by no matter what craftsman. Michelangelo received from Piero Soderini in payment for it four hundred crowns; and it was set in place in the year 1504.

Michelangelo was engaged to sculpt a figure of David in 1501 from a chunk of marble quarried a century earlier. David had always been the intended subject, but various sculptors had failed in even beginning to bring something out of the stone. After working mostly in secret, Michelangelo emerged after three years with the magnificent 17-foot figure that was nicknamed *Il Gigante*—"the Giant."

David was originally intended to be one of a group of figures that would perch high on the buttresses of the *Duomo*, the cathedral in Florence. However, on seeing the finished work, the Florentines decided that a better spot could and should be found, not only because the work was too massive to be practically and safely hoisted to the heights, but also because they wanted it to be more easily seen, perhaps in part as a symbol of Florence, which saw itself as a David amid the Goliaths of surrounding city-states. A group of artists and civic figures, including Leonardo da Vinci, met and determined that the best spot would be in front of the Palazzo Vecchio, where it stood for three centuries, until, for its own protection, it was moved into the Accademia museum.

And so these failures, missteps, and changing circumstances brought David into Michelangelo's life—and then, through him, into ours.

This fruit of Michelangelo's genius embodies, as Bishop Barron says, Renaissance humanism and its "celebration of the glory and beauty of the human being. Going beyond even the most skilled of his classical forebears, Michelangelo here depicts the symmetry, harmony, athleticism, and sheer grandeur of the human body."

During the Renaissance, artists and scientists wove rediscovered classical humanism with Christian sensibility, both explicitly and subtly. Michelangelo was, of course, a Catholic, and during the years he worked on *David*, he believed he was fashioning a sculpture that would stand atop a cathedral. Not, perhaps, as an intimate devotional object such as a statue of the Madonna in a niche, flickering with candles, or Stations of the Cross arrayed solemnly along shadowy walls, but with a clear spiritual import nonetheless.

For when Christians—whether we live in the sixteenth century or the twenty-first—consider David, great king of Israel, we also recall the One to whom the broken and blind called out as he passed by, "Son of David! Have pity on me!"

David foreshadows Jesus as king, ruler, and defender. The People of God eagerly awaited a successor to the great king, and the reestablishment of the kingdom—a Messiah whose rule would bring peace and healing. *Could this be the Messiah?* Many wondered as Jesus walked among them.

Even in David as a young man, in his unlikely battle against Goliath, Christian tradition has seen a foreshadowing of Jesus in battle against death and sin on the Cross, armed only with the power of God.

Most depictions of this event capture the moment after David's victory, usually with Goliath's head underfoot or in hand. Not here, though. Michelangelo brings us into the moment before—the moment, perhaps, of decision. David gazes intently, his brow furrowed, and his look is, from some angles, peaceful, but from others, intense and focused—in such a way that one participant in the placement committee thought such a menacing figure must be placed indoors, lest the Florentines think David was glaring at *them*.

And so Michelangelo's *David* stands, ready for battle. Nude, exposed to the powers of the world, trusting in God. Some have remarked that the sling strap across David's back could be reminiscent of the cross on the back of Christ. He stands on a rock with a tree stump to the rear of his right leg. This could, of course, be simply a practical choice on Michelangelo's part, to give the piece more support. But contemplating the figure of David, son of Jesse, emerging from out of that stump, we remember what Isaiah prophesied to a waiting, hopeful people:

> *But a shoot shall sprout from the stump of Jesse,*
> *and from his roots a bud shall blossom.*

The spirit of the LORD shall rest upon him:
a spirit of wisdom and of understanding,
A spirit of counsel and of strength,
a spirit of knowledge and of fear of the LORD.
(Isa 11:1-3)

Michelangelo brought a near-perfect human figure out of solid stone. As his contemporary, the art historian and biographer Giorgio Vasari, wrote in the excerpt above, *David* was so perfect, there was no need for anyone to ever bother with seeing any other sculpture of the human figure at all!

The artistic and expressive excellence is certainly admirable, but the "perfection" of *David* can point us to contemplation of a different sort, as well: a contemplation of Christ. As Bishop Barron says, "Christ is the son of David and he is the New Adam, the realization of what God has always intended for humanity. Think of the risen Jesus as the fulfillment of every possible human potential, spiritual and physical. Christianity does not advocate the escape of the soul from the body—as do Platonism and Gnosticism—but rather the resurrection and transfiguration of the body.... Looking at Jesus, Pontius Pilate said '*ecce homo*,' behold the man. With unconscious irony, Pilate was holding up the man he was condemning to death as the archetype of humanity. In this unparalleled sculpture of David, prototype of Christ, Michelangelo is saying much the same thing."

I am not perfect—and of course David, in actuality, was far from perfect himself. But this is the point. Jesus entered this imperfect world, took on weak flesh and redeemed it. He redeemed us. In Michelangelo's *David*, and looking further, in the Christ to whom David points us, we see the promise of redemption, a hint of what human beings were created to be, and, through assenting to his power and grace, can be.

<u>Consider:</u> *What flaws and limitations distort my nature as God created it? What sinful habits deepen this distortion? How open am I to change, repentance, and reform of my life?*

<u>Pray:</u> *Lord God, cleanse me of my sins. Take my will, fill me so that my life might reflect your goodness, beauty, glory, and perfection.*

MICHELANGELO

THE PIETÀ

Eternal Lord, eased of a cumbrous load,

And loosened from the world, I turn to thee;

Shun, like a shattered bark, the storm, and flee

To thy protection for a safe abode.

The crown of thorns, hands pierced upon the tree,

The meek, benign, and lacerated face,

To a sincere repentance promised grace,

To the sad soul give hope of pardon free.

With justice mark not thou, O Light divine,

My fault, nor hear it with thy sacred ear;

Neither put forth that way thy arm severe;

Wash with thy blood my sins; thereto incline

More readily the more my years require

Help, and forgiveness speedy and entire.

Michelangelo was not only a visual artist—he wrote poetry as well, a pastime that occupied many intellectuals of his time, no matter what their primary pursuit in life might be. It was fashionable to pen poetry, part of any good correspondent's repertoire.

Most of Michelangelo's poems were addressed to specific people or in their honor: patrons, friends, men and women whom he experienced as inspiring muses of one sort or another. During the latter part of his life, Michelangelo's poetry became more contemplative, spiritual, and even melancholy.

This poem, presented here in a translation by the nineteenth-century Romantic poet William Wordsworth, was written when Michelangelo was an old man. The *Pietà* that stands in Saint Peter's Basilica was sculpted when he was only in his early twenties. Perhaps sixty years separate the sculpting of the mother holding her Son and Michelangelo's reflection on the Death that placed the Son there. Both invite us to open our lives to merciful love.

In the *Pietà*, a youthful-appearing Mary cradles Jesus on her lap. Why does Michelangelo present Mary with a visage that looks no older than that of her son? Michelangelo himself answered that question by saying, "but don't you know that chaste women always preserve their youthful looks more than unchaste women?" It is a spiritual and theological point that Michelangelo is making here: Mary is the new Eve and ever-young mother of the Church.

And so she cradles her son—the figure of Mary is actually larger than that of Jesus, aided by her voluminous robes. Her outstretched left hand hints at presentation. We stand before the two of them, and, as we contemplate, Mary's hand suggests that here, in this moment, she is offering her Son to us, and even this has a number of layers and dimensions.

One of the many ways to think of Mary that has emerged through Christian history is the title of "Ark of the Covenant." The ark, in the context of Israel, was the structure that contained the tablets of the Decalogue, or Ten Commandments. It was understood to be, in a mysterious way, the actual dwelling place of God. At one point, King David goes to retrieve the ark, but realizes his (and Israel's) unworthiness, saying, "How can the ark of the Lord come into my care?" As he later accompanies the ark into Jerusalem with celebration, he speaks of being blessed by the presence of the ark (2 Sam 6:9-14). As is always the case, Christians pondered this Old Testament narrative, and saw the hand of God throughout all of Jewish and Christian tradition, weaving meaning and revelation. They pondered how, when Elizabeth greets Mary, she says, "How is that the Mother of the Lord comes to me?" In Elizabeth's greeting to Mary, they heard echoes of David's cry and, naturally enough, saw a new ark, bearing a new manifestation of God's protective, loving, powerful presence: Mary, the new ark of the new covenant.

Within her, all of God's creative power is recapitulated and evoked, not in buildings or mountains, but in a Person.

And here, she presents him to us.

In this moment, in contrast to the innumerable expressions of this theme in depictions of the Madonna and Child, the Son she cradles is lifeless. The scene expresses the human bond of grief and loss, but also makes a statement of faith. For the Christians in front of the scene know that indeed, we are offered the Body of Christ, as food for our souls, as nourishment for eternal life.

Jesus was born in Bethlehem, which means "House of Bread," and was placed by his mother in a manger, the place where animals eat. Through his death and resurrection, Jesus becomes food for the life of the world, for the redemption of all of creation. In the mystery of her heart pierced with sorrow, as Simeon prophesied, the Blessed Mother presents us with the Body of her Son Jesus, the Bread of Life.

Decades later, Michelangelo continues to reflect on Christ's death, this time in words. Near the end of a rich lifetime he writes, aware of his sins and the imprisoning burden of his worldly life. He brings all of this to the crucified Christ, not in fear or terror, but in regret, and above all in trusting hope.

Reflecting on our sins can be a depressing exercise. Reflecting on our mortality can be intensely, even fearfully sobering.

As well it should be, on both counts. Sin and death are serious, and our stance on both influences our daily decisions, which in turn, shapes the trajectory of our lives.

We may wonder sometimes what can be done about our bad choices, our sins, our harmful actions and habits. We carry the burden of the past, and it weighs us down, shrinking our vision as we are focused on our own heaviness rather than on the needs of a hurting world. We are afraid to admit our sins, afraid of confessing them, afraid—even as we yearn for it—of change.

We are just…afraid.

Michelangelo, in the *Pietà*, sculpted an encounter with sin and death—*the* encounter, perhaps. And in the cool stone, I see more than just magnificent artistic skill. I see God's answer… God has said yes to us, and given a way to move on, in trust and hope. The Loving Mother offers her Son to us; she offers, gently, God's answer to my sins: mercy.

Consider: *Images of death are deeply woven into Christian imagery. Why is this? How does this differ from how death is dealt with in contemporary culture? What does Michelangelo's Pietà say to me about sin, death, and hope?*

Pray: *Loving God, in my sin and mortality, I come to you. I pray for mercy and I pray for hope and trust in your love for me.*

MICHELANGELO

The Sistine Chapel

Beauty, whether that of the natural universe or that expressed in art, precisely because it opens up and broadens the horizons of human awareness, pointing us beyond ourselves, bringing us face to face with the abyss of Infinity, can become a path towards the transcendent, towards the ultimate Mystery, towards God. Art, in all its forms, at the point where it encounters the great questions of our existence, the fundamental themes that give life its meaning, can take on a religious quality, thereby turning into a path of profound inner reflection and spirituality.

The way of beauty leads us, then, to grasp the Whole in the fragment, the Infinite in the finite, God in the history of humanity.

We can examine any piece of art and study the skill, the formal composition, the color, and the contrast. But the Sistine Chapel frescoes were not painted as a gallery installation, and Michelangelo would undoubtedly be shocked at the sight of millions of yearly visitors flowing through the space, craning their necks to study the now well-lit frescoes.

For in considering these paintings, we cannot forget that Michelangelo painted the ceiling (and wall, in his *Last Judgment* behind the altar) of a *chapel*: specifically, the pope's chapel, in which Mass was offered and a new successor of Peter would be elected.

The narrative that Michelangelo presents—and it is a narrative that the eye can follow across the ceiling—concerns the coming of the savior, Christ, the new Adam prophesied by both pagan and Jewish figures in the surrounding panels. It is his incarnation that would reconcile matter and spirit and thereby repair the damage done by sin. Christ would do this via the sacrifice re-presented in the Mass—the experience of which would, in Michelangelo's understanding, be the primary reason anyone would be in the chapel in the first place, under the frescoes of the creation and the fall—not to stroll in, taking in the obligatory sites in between gelatos. Michelangelo envisioned viewers prayerfully mindful of their own sins, hopeful for mercy, entering into the reconciling sacrifice of Christ in the Mass.

The ceiling's nine primary panels depict scenes from the Old Testament, but are centered on Christ. They tell the story of why humanity needs the salvation that Christ gives through his death and resurrection, made accessible to believers every time that the Mass is offered.

The nine central panes can be divided into three triads, the first of which depicts the creation of the world: God's separation of light and darkness, then the creation of the sun, moon, planets, and earth, and finally a scene of God hovering over the sea, perhaps creating the creatures that teem, unseen.

The second triad deals with the creation of man and woman. The first pane reveals the iconic image, of course, of God creating Adam. We are so familiar with the image, we might take for granted that we understand it, just as we might half-listen to Scripture readings we have heard proclaimed our entire lives. But the details, all purposeful on Michelangelo's part, express notes that might surprise and certainly deepen our understanding not only of the work itself, but of creation, redemption, and, hence, ourselves.

We might wonder, first of all, how this panel can be described as the "creation" of Adam, when there he is, lying on a cloud, already existing. A common interpretation of this point is that what Michelangelo is presenting is the moment that God is infusing Adam with a soul or imparting to him the *imago Dei*—the defining aspect of humanity through which we are made "in the image of God"—our intelligence, will, imagination, freedom, and, of course, our spiritual nature and soul.

God is concentrating on that finger, expressive of the ancient Christian association between the Holy Spirit and the finger of God. Saint Augustine put it this way: "the Holy Spirit, through whom charity is shed abroad in our hearts, is also called in the Gospel the finger of God.... God's finger is God's spirit through whom we are sanctified.... The same spirit of God that hovered over the waters now communicates life to human beings."

Look, too, if you can, at God's other hand. It, too, is pointing, in a way, that extended finger, touching the shoulder of a child. The child is positioned in a way that clearly echoes Adam's position, his facial features similar as well, and he is next to a woman who is, in turn, huddled under the Creator's left arm—Eve, and the Child indicated by God is Jesus, the Son of Man who will redeem all. As Saint Paul writes:

> *He is the image of the invisible God, the firstborn of all creation; for in him all things in heaven and on earth were created, things visible and invisible, whether thrones or dominions or rulers or powers— all things have been created through him and for him. He himself is before all things, and in him all things hold together. (Col 15:17)*

The central panel depicts the creation of Eve, who emerges from Adam and is moving in a prayerful, adoring stance towards the Creator. In contrast, in the next panel, which is a scene of the Fall, both Adam and Eve move away from the garden, their formerly strong, beautiful figures now distorted and hunched closer to the earth, rather than reaching towards God.

The final three panels concern the effects of original sin, as recounted in the story of Noah. Michelangelo depicts the corruption of sin, the Flood itself, and, finally, the humiliation of Noah by his children. This unfamiliar story may seem like an odd choice, but remember that in that moment, worldly spirits—drink—have robbed Noah of his mind, will, and responsibility, and made him a parody of what God created human beings to be—a condition visually depicted in Noah's pose, a faint, sad, lifeless echo of Adam's in the creation scene.

As Bishop Barron notes: "Though this cycle ends on a negative note, we are not meant to be discouraged, for the entire purpose of the narrative is to make sense of the coming of the Savior, who by his incarnation would reconcile matter and spirit, and thereby repair the damage done by sin. Christ, the new Adam, would come to undo the effects of the fall."

It is all about hope—*real* hope, the hope found in Christ, which is, in turn, available to all of the broken, the sinful, the damaged, through the very Body of Christ offered amidst these powerful images. The trust and hope that the beauty of humanity expressed in Michelangelo's images are but a faint image of what our loving, merciful God has in store for those who love him.

Consider: *The history of salvation is the history of all of us. Created by a loving God, sinful, redeemed. What truths do Michelangelo's frescos reveal about human life, fallenness, and hope?*

Pray: *Heavenly Father, you created me out of love, for eternal life with you. I ask for forgiveness for my sins, grace to overcome what keeps me from you, and trust in your mercy through Christ.*

ST. THOMAS AQUINAS

THEOLOGY AND SPIRITUALITY

Part I, Question 1, Article 1. Whether, besides philosophy, any further doctrine is required?

I answer that, It was necessary for man's salvation that there should be a knowledge revealed by God besides philosophical science built up by human reason. Firstly, indeed, because man is directed to God, as to an end that surpasses the grasp of his reason: "The eye hath not seen, O God, besides thee, what things thou hast prepared for them that wait for thee" (Isa 64:4). But the end must first be known by men who are to direct their thoughts and actions to the end. Hence it was necessary for the salvation of man that certain truths which exceed human reason should be made known to him by divine revelation.... Therefore, in order that the salvation of men might be brought about more fitly and more surely, it was necessary that they should be taught divine truths by divine revelation. It was therefore necessary that besides philosophical science built up by reason, there should be a sacred science learned through revelation.

We ask questions about faith as soon as we can talk and think about it. As children we tried to imagine God; as young people we marveled—and perhaps even worried—about the vastness of the universe, our place in it, and God's role in the whole thing. As adults, the questions still keep coming, and they are not a mark of a lack of faith any more than seeking to know a best friend or spouse more intimately is a sign of a lack of love.

But how to answer the questions? Is having faith dependent on answering them in a way that is satisfactorily rational to the modern mind? Or should we even bother, convinced, as some would have us be, that the only answer that matters is what we "feel" or what is "in our hearts"?

Saint Thomas Aquinas asked questions, and answered them in an exhaustive way, unafraid of any corner of human wisdom, convinced—as is the entire Catholic tradition—that faith and reason, both rooted in divine wisdom, can never conflict.

Saint Thomas teaches us to plunge into questions, open to truth, which means open to God.

But what of these questions Thomas asks, beginning, let's say, with the passage above? It seems quite technical. The writing is almost a thousand years old. What does it have in common with *my* questions *today*? And, just as importantly, my faith?

In this passage from the *Summa theologiae*, his massive examination of almost any God-question one could think of, Thomas explains—in the context of medieval academics—why philosophy is not sufficient for explaining reality. Quite simply, the reason why is that human beings have been created by God for eternal life with God. This dimension of life is not unreasonable, but it lies beyond reason. The truth about that dimension that every soul was created for and yearns for on this earth is rooted in revelation. Theology explores it: why we exist, who we are, and where we are going. It engages the deepest questions of our hearts using reason.

Every time I wonder if I really do need to take religion and faith seriously, every time I live as if human wisdom and achievement—mine and that of the world I live in—is enough, I'm asking this very question. And Saint Thomas has an answer for me.

Now, the practice of theology can, like any other aspect of religious life, be drained of life and faith, in need of a regular brisk reorientation and reminder that our intellectual efforts and achievements are not God—only God is God.

But to dismiss theology as an unnecessary aspect of Christian life or even an obstacle to authentic spirituality would be wrong as well. It might even be ironic that the figure to point that out to us with great power is the theologian very often and most unfairly associated with negative judgments of theology: Saint Thomas Aquinas himself.

So, if we look at the passage above, Thomas concludes that theology exists, not to "prove" points, construct fine-sounding arguments, or overwhelm the doubter with words, but, as he says explicitly, for the cause of human "salvation." Thomas is a spiritual master whose writings were designed to lead people to Christ.

This understanding of the role of theology in the disciples' life is seen nowhere more clearly than in the life of Thomas himself. After decades of work, the deeply devout, indefatigable scholar had a mystical experience at Mass after which he reportedly retired his writing tools and said, "all I have written seems like straw to me."

This is not—we think—a dismissal of his life's work. For when one reads Thomas' life work, what we find are not words written for their own sake or for the pleasure of an intricately woven argument, much less for academic advancement. What we read is evoked in the passage above: a profound love and concern for souls. For Thomas, theology is a *via*—a way to lead souls to God.

Catholicism is not all theology. It is *caritas*—love poured out as Jesus poured himself out. It is sacrament, communion, art, family life, religious life, the saints. It is all of this and more, but what we can't help but notice is that even these seemingly uncomplicated aspects of the disciples' lives lead to questions. What is "love," and what is it proper for me to love and in what way? How does Jesus come to meet me through the sacraments of his Body, the Church? How do I know that the Scriptures I'm supposed to be living by are God's Word? If God is all-good, why do evil and seemingly unjust suffering exist? How can I sense God's movement and will in the world, in my own life? And what is the difference? Theological questions, every one of them.

So our own spiritual lives, like Thomas', call for balance. Emphasizing the intellect too much, I find a cave in which to hide, avoid relationship and communion with God and others. But in disparaging theology, I reject the life of the mind, a mind created by God to seek him and know him, just as much as my heart is. I may even avoid tough questions, not just because they are challenging, but because I'm a little bit afraid of the answers. Theological reflection from people with deep understanding helps me. It opens me to the truth that God is more than what I feel or personally experience, and this "more" matters a great deal.

Thomas himself was balanced. He prayed the Mass with intense devotion, wrote beautiful hymns, sacrificed much to give himself wholly to God, and delighted in using the intellect God had given him to fearlessly explore challenging questions.

The great American fiction writer Flannery O'Connor was a Georgia-born Catholic who died of lupus at the age of 38. In one of her letters—invaluable spiritual reading—she shared her own affection for Thomas, and how he had shaped not just her mind, but her whole life as a Christian:

> *I couldn't make any judgment on the Summa,*
> *except to say this: I read it every night before I go*

to bed. *If my mother were to come in during the process and say, "Turn off that light. It's late," I, with lifted finger and broad, bland, beatific expression, would reply, "On the contrary, I answer that the light, being eternal and limitless, cannot be turned off. Shut your eyes," or some such thing. In any case I feel I can personally guarantee that Saint Thomas loved God because for the life of me I cannot help loving Saint Thomas.*

Consider: *What theological questions particularly vex me? When I have theological questions, where do I seek answers?*

Pray: *God of Wisdom, you have gifted me with a mind to know you. Open my mind to seek truth with greater courage and trust.*

ST. THOMAS AQUINAS

THE EXISTENCE OF GOD

Part I, Question 2, Article 3. Whether God exists?

I answer that the existence of God can be proved in five ways.

The first and more manifest way is the argument from motion. It is certain, and evident to our senses, that in the world some things are in motion.... Whatever is in motion must be put in motion by another. If that by which it is put in motion be itself put in motion, then this also must needs be put in motion by another, and that by another again. But this cannot go on to infinity, because then there would be no first mover, and, consequently, no other mover; seeing that subsequent movers move only inasmuch as they are put in motion by the first mover; as the staff moves only because it is put in motion by the hand. Therefore it is necessary to arrive at a first mover, put in motion by no other; and this everyone understands to be God.

Most of us had our first meeting with Saint Thomas Aquinas in two areas: his hymns and prayers, such as the *Tantum Ergo* sung at benediction, and his "proofs" for the existence of God.

We do commonly call them "proofs," but the better term would be Thomas' own—*viae*, or "ways." We might have found them helpful in discussions with unbelievers and doubters—groups that might even include ourselves from time to time. They're good for pointing out that belief in God is not irrational or contrary to the evidence of the natural world, and in fact is a reasonable conclusion from our observations of that same world.

And apologetics rooted in these demonstrations is great. But reflecting on Saint Thomas' five ways can be spiritually clarifying and bracing for any of us. My spirituality is about prayer and mindfulness, about inviting God in, about communion with God that touches every part of my day, making my entire life my spiritual life. Meditating on Saint Thomas' five ways clarifies what that means, and—always so important in Thomas' thought—what it *doesn't* mean.

Thomas' *viae* derive from observations of the natural world, informed by Aristotle. He writes that we can know that God exists and something important about God by the fact of motion (there must be an unmoved mover to get everything started); causation (everything has a cause, so there must be a first cause); possibility and necessity (all of creation is contingent, so there must be being that does not receive its existence from another being); gradation of being (some things are better or worse than others, therefore there must be a best, a standard), and design (things exist towards a goal, so there must be a mind setting that direction, as an archer directs an arrow).

These five ways have been discussed and dissected for centuries, with strengths and weaknesses highlighted by believers and skeptics alike. But in addition to what Thomas' *viae* teach us about the chain of being, they also reveal a profound spiritual truth about those of us pondering them: They all basically come down to the cold, hard truth that we are not sufficient unto ourselves.

We sometimes forget this. Assuming, even subconsciously, that we have only ourselves to thank for our own existence, we begin to live that way, and it's interesting to consider the disparate but connected fruits of this forgetting: pride and despair.

When I create a world that I was born into randomly, which operates either arbitrarily or out of my own power, there is no reason to be grateful. My meaning is my own, derived from my own needs and wants. I am proud, but I am alone.

When I create a world in which there is nothing "behind" me, as it were, in which everything I do *must* come out of my own power, in which I *must* create my own meaning, crowded on all sides by other creatures engaged in the same confusing, unending project, I find myself wondering if I can possibly be worth anything, if there is any purpose in anything any of us are up to, for anything we put our trust in certainly fades away. In this cacophony of self-generation and constant low hum of yearning, I my find myself in despair, and I am alone.

But Saint Thomas' *viae* assure us—or warn us—of this: we are, in fact, not alone at all. We have not placed ourselves here; we have not decided to exist; we have not caused ourselves. We are not the ultimate ground of our existence; we do not have ourselves to thank for that.

It is God we have to thank.

It's a warning. It's an enormous relief. And, ultimately, it is profoundly freeing.

The careful, smart ideas of Saint Thomas—grounded in the great philosophers, the best science of his day, and, of course, divine revelation—don't wrap up God in a flawless package and hand him to us. For Thomas wants us to understand above all that God is not a fellow creature or even a "being" alongside other beings. No, what they do is shake us, identifying not only the hints of the divine ground of all existence in the shape, movement, direction, and design of creation, but identifying just as importantly the pride that blinds us to those signs and the sad, bitter fruit—grasped so eagerly from that tree—of the pride.

For Thomas knows this about himself, and about you and me: "Disciples must first be shaken out of their own self-complacency and tendency to cling to their egos, then shaken out of their immersion of the passing things of the world, and finally stirred out of their allegiance to the mighty and permanent powers that are yet less than God. Each step in the proof represents a re-orienting intervention of the spiritual director, a call continually to look higher.... In these proofs, he shows us that in the roots of our being we are in relation to a reality that is utterly unlike the finite and contingent things of the world, that we are in the saving grasp of something stranger than we can possibly imagine."

Consider: *What reminders of my dependence on God have I experienced? What in my daily life recalls God's power over me?*

Pray: *Lord of life and the universe, may the life you have given me be lived in profound gratitude and praise.*

ST. THOMAS AQUINAS

THE NATURE OF GOD

Part I, Question 3, Article 4. Whether essence and existence are the same in God?

I answer that, God is not only his own essence, as shown in the preceding article, but also his own existence. This may be shown in several ways.

First, whatever a thing has besides its essence must be caused either by the constituent principles of that essence...or by some exterior agent—as heat is caused in water by fire. Therefore, if the existence of a thing differs from its essence, this existence must be caused either by some exterior agent or by its essential principles. Now it is impossible for a thing's existence to be caused by its essential constituent principles, for nothing can be the sufficient cause of its own existence, if its existence is caused. Therefore that thing, whose existence differs from its essence, must have its existence caused by another. But this cannot be true of God, because we call God the first efficient cause. Therefore it is impossible that in God his existence should differ from his essence.

At the beginning of every discussion in the *Summa* stands a question. After the questions come possible answers that Saint Thomas then bats around between varied viewpoints, echoing the intense university discussions that made up the daily life of a professor.

Once again, a question like this brings up questions of its own. It's pretty philosophical, and also seems pretty far from the realities of my own life. How can a discussion about God's essence and existence possibly matter? What difference would the answer to this incredibly technical question make, anyway?

Well, what *are* my questions? In terms of God, perhaps they are similar to yours. Who is God? How can I find God, be sure it is God I have found, and *remain* in God? Here is my life. Here is yours. Here is the universe. How are we connected to God?

Those questions are persistent, and throughout our lives, we work out various answers. Our responses depend on so many things: our family lives, our culture, our own personal qualities, our experiences, what we're taught, and even our fears. Even if we don't explicitly ask them, our decisions and priorities indicate that we are, in some sense, answering them nonetheless.

Our answers have strengths and weaknesses and, varied relationships to the truth. Walking with Saint Thomas and considering these complicated ideas the best we can might help us avoid a few particularly dangerous weaknesses, though. For one of the greatest dangers in the spiritual life involves reducing God to our own terms, as a fellow being—bigger and more powerful perhaps, but still, in the end, constructed in our image—objectified and pulled out of hiding only when convenient or not too much of a threat, and rejected when his ways seem to conflict with our ways.

All of Saint Thomas' discussions of God, rooted as they are in revelation, tradition, and reason, come back again and again to one thing: the notion of *divine simplicity*. God is, we must understand and admit before anything else, *simple*.

By this Thomas does not mean that God is shallow or easy to understand. Of course not. Rather, he means that God is not a kind or type of being, like you, I, or this book, but is rather the *act of being itself*, without distinction, specification, or condition.

One of those distinctions is between essence (what a thing is) and existence (the fact that it is). All created things have this distinction. This book is a being (it exists) with an essence of "bookness." It is a thing that has being. God— as Thomas explains in the excerpt above—does not have this distinction, a truth so simply and powerfully articulated in God's announcement of his name to Moses from the burning bush: *I AM WHO AM.* His essence is his existence.

Through the *Summa*, Thomas explores many other attributes of God, attributes that are really, when you think about them, negations. He explains how God is infinite—without borders and outside time. God is immutable—he cannot be improved upon.

In other words, God is not out there, in competition with other beings, including me.

God is here, continually creating and knowing.

So yes, these complicated notions about the radical simplicity of God matter to us as we make our way through a world with barriers thrown up at every turn—from birth, it seems—between us and the loving one who graciously called us into being.

I am challenged to reconsider my response to God as I take this all in. I have to ask myself if I really pray—no, do I really *live* in a way that is mindful and faithful to this truth? Or do I imagine (or even hope) that there are parts of me that are unavailable to God because I can hide them?

Do I hesitate in my prayer because I am convinced that there are parts of life simply too unimportant for God's attention, too insignificant for God to care about?

Have I separated my life into sections, inviting God into some but shutting him out of others, declaring that those particular decisions have nothing to do with faith?

Do I live with the suspicion or even the conviction that my sins have cut me off from God?

On a brisk, windy night, I walk outside and consider, in astonishment, that everything I see—and what is more, everything I cannot see—all things visible and invisible—spring from God, and in some way, rest in God, are dependent on God, who is utterly simple.

What Saint Thomas' life work tells me is this: *It matters who God is*. God is not a figment of my imagination. God isn't one thing for you and another for me. It is difficult to talk about God—every saint knows this. But every saint also knows that it is very important to not say false things about God. If the truth about God doesn't matter at all, then spirituality becomes a self-referential feedback loop that usually ends up supporting our negative tendencies.

So what Thomas teaches me is important because of my limited vision, my pride, and my self-referential nature—in short, my sin. Not all idols are made of wood or metal. There are more ways to limit God than simply constraining his power to a statue.

When Saint Paul preached to the Athenians, he accused their hand-carved gods of being limited, in contrast to the God of Jesus Christ:

The God who made the world and everything in it, he who is Lord of heaven and earth, does not live in shrines made by human hands, nor is he served by human hands, as though he needed anything, since he himself gives to all mortals life and breath and all things. From one ancestor he made all nations to inhabit the whole earth, and he allotted the times of their existence and the boundaries of the places where they would live, so that they would search for God and perhaps grope for him and find him—though indeed he is not far from each one of us. For "In him we live and move and have our being..."
(Acts 17:24-28)

Consider: *What are some areas of my life from which I exclude God? How would life look different if I understood God's presence throughout all of it?*

Pray: *Loving God, you have probed me and you know me. You knew me before I was born. May I welcome your loving presence, and no longer run from it.*

ST. THOMAS AQUINAS

THE HUMAN PERSON

Part IIa, Question 2, Article 8. Whether any created good constitutes man's happiness?

It is impossible for any created good to constitute man's happiness. For happiness is the perfect good, which lulls the appetite altogether; else it would not be the last end, if something yet remained to be desired. Now the object of the will, i.e., of man's appetite, is the universal good; just as the object of the intellect is the universal true. Hence it is evident that nothing can lull man's will, save the universal good. This is to be found, not in any creature, but in God alone; because every creature has goodness by participation. Wherefore God alone can satisfy the will of man.

What I want to do, what I need to do, what I can't and shouldn't do. How to love, to serve, when to say yes, when to say no and turn away.

When I awake in the morning, I ponder these questions—if I give myself time and can shake off my sleep—and I sketch them out, for the day, at least.

Hours later, it's evening, and time for the examination of conscience. Regret, confession, hope. Cautious optimism, more questions. Wondering if I can continue on the path I know is the right one, the path that leads me into closer communion with God, wondering if it's worth the sacrifice.

Reading the Scriptures, listening to the saints, I discover that none of this is new, none of it is unique to my experience. Saint Paul writes of being torn: "For I know that nothing good dwells within me, that is, in my flesh. I can will what is right, but I cannot do it. For I do not do the good I want, but the evil I do not want is what I do" (Rom 7:18-19).

Spiritual writers from Augustine to Thomas Merton dissected the divided heart that finds delight in created things, certainly gifts from God, but yearns always for more, and for a more that never ends.

Saint Thomas knew this as well, and his discussion of the human person reflects this keen awareness of the tension of the journey all of us are on. Again, his treatment seems so technical, so distant from the contemporary language that invites me to be my "best self" and "discern my gifts and talents," as if that were a simple thing. For we always come back to the question—when it comes to myself, whom can I trust? My decisions about my life must be based on *something*—on some sense of who I am, what I'm about, and why I am here. What is the truth about me and the rest of humanity? Who are we supposed to be?

The *Summa theologiae* begins with God, but turns quickly to creation, then specifically to the human person. Thomas takes time first to explain the intimate, necessary connection between body and soul. I am not a soul trapped inside a body, waiting for the moment of release to be truly free. No, creatures are body and soul.

This truth impacts my journey of discernment in a few ways. I'm reminded that my body matters, and that my relationship with God and his creation is mediated through that body.

My bodily self matters in another way as well: my soul—my entire self—is impacted by how I live in this body on this earthly plane. I can't separate the two and pretend that I can do whatever I feel like and it somehow won't affect my spirit. I am one piece, and I can't forget that in the Apostle's Creed, I proclaim that I believe in the "resurrection of the body." My body has been a single cell, my body has been young and strong, and my body will someday—if I make it that far—be aged, worn, and sick. All of that is me, integrally, and not just as a spaceship for my soul. All of that was Jesus of Nazareth, who redeemed it and sanctified it from beginning to end.

I have to consider, honestly, if I believe in this intimate unity and dynamic between body and soul. My habits of eating, drinking, physical intimacy, my speech, my treatment of others, my use of time. What I have done and what I have failed to do with the body Christ has sanctified. Do I live in this body as if I believe it has been sanctified by Christ?

Discerning along these lines often evokes the question, "why?" Why do I persist in these sins? Why do I keep saying "yes" to using my body for less than Christlike purposes? Why do I avoid using my brain, talents, time, mouth, hands, feet, and sight for the possible good right in front of me, which really does not ask that much of me, if I am honest.

Here, too, Thomas has an answer for me. It's quoted above, and it comes down to this: scientists of all sorts have all kinds of things to say about us, human beings. Where we come from and why we do what we do, and even how to change us. What they say might be true or false, but none of it, even the true parts, goes as deeply as Saint Thomas does. Rooted in what God has revealed through Scripture and developed through tradition, Thomas reminds me of how important it is to know who I am.

A creature, yes, but a special sort of creature. One made in the *imago Dei*, in God's image.

In Genesis we read that, after all the other creatures had been fashioned, God did something different: "So God created humankind in his image, in the image of God he created them; male and female he created them" (Gen 1:27).

We are different from other creatures. God has shared with us the capacity for free will, for creativity, for communion, for reason. He created us for life with him. All those deep hungers that drive us? Examining them closely, we—along with spiritual masters throughout history, for there is nothing particularly contemporary about this observation—see that in all of them, we are living out a yearning for God.

What this does not mean—and here is where discernment that goes beyond feelings and into truth comes in—is that everything I do is good and God-directed just because I do it. Therein lies a dangerous temptation: to rationalize my sinful tendencies, habits, and choices as spiritually sound because I *think* I am spiritually sound, I pray, I go to church, and I know God loves me. People fall into this. Religious institutions fall into it, which is one more reason why the objective nature of an inquiry such as Saint Thomas' is so important in discerning the divine life, goodness, and beauty that we are seeking even sometimes in the midst of sin.

As Bishop Barron writes elsewhere, "we are nothing but hunger and thirst for the divine life. Every energy, every power, every thought and action of ours is, explicitly or implicitly, animated by the divine power, drawn by it and determined by it."

We seek. We seek love and acceptance. We seek knowledge. We seek *life*.

Consider: *What are my deepest yearnings? What good do those yearnings reflect? Are they properly or improperly directed?*

Pray: *Creator God, you made me for you. Deep within, I bear your image. Form me so that all my thoughts and actions are consciously directed to you and your will for me.*

CHRIST

Part III, Question 1, Article 1. Whether it was fitting that God should become incarnate?

It would seem most fitting that by visible things the invisible things of God should be made known; for to this end was the whole world made, as is clear from the word of the Apostle (Rom 1:20): "For the invisible things of God...are clearly seen, being understood by the things that are made." But, as Damascene says, by the mystery of Incarnation are made known at once the goodness, the wisdom, the justice, and the power or might of God—"His goodness, for he did not despise the weakness of his own handiwork; his justice, since, on man's defeat, he caused the tyrant to be overcome by none other than man, and yet he did not snatch men forcibly from death; his wisdom, for he found a suitable discharge for a most heavy debt; his power, or infinite might, for there is nothing greater than for God to become incarnate..."

I was recently in a coffee shop, trying to pound out a few words, while a kid was taking a midterm exam. It was quiet at first, but as the morning wore on, the customers poured in.

An African-American man in a black suit, red shoes, red tie, and red fedora, sat taking notes from a Bible.

A middle-aged white man with close-cropped gray hair and hipster glasses was doing the same.

101

It struck me that both men were probably preparing sermons or Sunday School classes.

There was a group of runners. I tried not to despise them. Students with their books. Other students back from college, high school friends, reunited, catching up, and exchanging gifts. Business men and women rushing in for their lattes, intense conversations, boisterous greetings.

Watching it all from a table near the register, a homeless fellow sat, newspapers spread out, black plastic garbage bag at his feet, knit cap, lips moving, staring, nodding. He's a regular, it seemed, for he was not left out of the morning greetings, either.

Here we all are, along with everyone else on the planet. Bank tellers five doors down, the toy store owner across the road, children at school a couple of blocks away. Cooks and dishwashers, construction workers, doctors, mourners gathering at the nearby parish for the funeral of the young mother who died of melanoma, her husband, their three children under five. Here we are, building things, wrecking them, making sense, being ridiculous, reaching out, slamming doors in rage. Here we are in the womb, in hospitals, thriving, suffering, fighting, dying.

Is it fitting that God should become incarnate?

No, says the skeptical observer. We are too messy, too small, too wrong.

Yes, says Saint Thomas. Absolutely. It is indeed the most fitting, the most God-like thing God can do to join himself to our worn-out, worrisome flesh.

And this is why: God's nature is to be good. Goodness is characterized by a generosity and a going out of oneself. As

Thomas points out in this passage, since God is the highest good, he gives himself in the fullest manner. This is what happens when he joins himself to his own creation.

God, as Bishop Barron says, is characterized by an ecstatic love, moving towards the other. The reason Saint Thomas writes that "there is nothing greater than for God to become incarnate" is that no "mere" being—even a "supreme" being—could do such a thing and remain true to itself. It is, then, only in Christ that we see this highest sort of self-expression, of self-emptying.

And in that—in the Incarnation into the boundaries of creation—do we see how good and loving God is.

But what of us? Who are we? These creatures whose poor flesh God has so lovingly, graciously, and even shockingly taken on? We who are loved?

The Incarnation reveals the answer to that question, too.

Humanity, made by God for God, created with the capacity to be in communion with him now and forever, reaches for the divine life, and in Christ is utterly taken up into that for which it reaches.

What do I see when I contemplate the mysterious, fully divine and fully human nature of Christ? I see humility and surrender, obedience and loving sacrifice. I see deep, utter, and complete freedom. I see what God created and invites human beings to be—which is why, from early on, Jesus was referred to as the "New Adam"—in him humanity is redeemed, saved from sin, and restored.

I see, as Bishop Barron writes elsewhere, "the meeting of divine and human self-forgetting…the proper human stance vis-à-vis

God, that attitude of obedience, openness, and self-transcending love that alone allows the fullness of the divine to emerge."

We see this mystery lived out in the entire life of Christ, from the grace of his virginal conception and the Incarnation, through his teaching and miracles, to, most powerfully, his Passion, Death, and Resurrection. We center our churches on a crucifix, we hang a crucifix on the walls of our homes, we wear them around our necks for a reason.

In that icon of a man hanging on a cross, God reveals who he is and who we are called to be.

As Pope Benedict XVI said on Good Friday in 2008:

> *This is the truth of Good Friday: on the Cross, the Redeemer has restored to us the dignity that belongs to us, has made us adoptive sons and daughters of God whom he has created in his image and likeness. Let us remain, then, in adoration before the Cross. O Christ, crucified King, give us true knowledge of you, the joy for which we yearn, the love that fills our heart, thirsty for the infinite. This is our prayer for this evening, Jesus, Son of God, who died for us on the Cross and was raised up on the third day.*

There are times that we sense our lives have veered off course or even gotten out of control. External events can certainly do that to us. Being mired in a rut, struggling to even get by, takes its toll on us. Bored, restless, fearful, and worried—where do I turn? What has happened? What does it mean to be a person right now, or ever? Visit your average coffee shop and you'll see how different everyone is. What could possibly bind us?

My feelings may tell me one thing. In fact, they may tell me one thing today and another tomorrow. But the spiritual importance of what Saint Thomas and all of Catholic tradition tells me is, frankly, that my feelings on the matter are not the point. There is a true thing about me and everyone else on the planet, and the truth is that in Jesus Christ, God reveals his utter goodness and ecstatic love, and we are the object of that love. *Us.*

Knowing this about God, about myself, and about the world makes a difference. It matters. It means that, as I sit in a coffee shop, I see this little world differently. I see every person as created and beloved by God. It doesn't matter how I feel about it, either. It is just the truth. A truth about love that knows no boundaries, which calls me to a wonder-filled, grateful openness to that love, poured out in Christ, right now, right where we are.

Consider: *How much of my sense of self and others is formed by an understanding of being created by God in his image and redeemed by Christ? How can I deepen this understanding, and what might it change to do so?*

Pray: *Loving God, you brought all of us into being. In gratitude for life and the grace of the Incarnation, may my communion with others deepen, my compassion broaden, and my love know no boundaries.*

G.K. CHESTERTON

Joy

Man is more himself, man is more manlike, when joy is the fundamental thing in him, and grief the superficial. Melancholy should be an innocent interlude, a tender and fugitive frame of mind; praise should be the permanent pulsation of the soul. Pessimism is at best an emotional half-holiday; joy is the uproarious labor by which all things live. Yet, according to the apparent estate of man as seen by the pagan or the agnostic, this primary need of human nature can never be fulfilled. Joy ought to be expansive; but for the agnostic it must be contracted, it must cling to one corner of the world.... Christianity satisfies suddenly and perfectly man's ancestral instinct for being the right way up; satisfies it supremely in this: that by its creed joy becomes something gigantic and sadness something special and small.... We can take our own tears more lightly than we could take the tremendous levities of the angels. So we sit perhaps in a starry chamber of silence, while the laughter of the heavens is too loud for us to hear.

What is joy?

In a superficial culture cut off from the transcendent, "joy" sometimes seems to be about not much more than a grin, lots of noise, and continual expressions of cheerfulness and good will, no matter how difficult the circumstances.

Well, Saint Paul exhorts the Philippians to "Rejoice...always." Is this any different? Just as his call to "pray without ceasing" can puzzle us, so can this. Life interrupts, life is hard, life is sad. Who has the time or emotional strength to be happy all the time? It seems like an irritating and delusional way of life.

Although G.K. Chesterton is certainly remembered for his cheerfulness and his optimistic yet realistic outlook, we can see even from the excerpt above, from his classic book *Orthodoxy*, that the call to joy is more complex than simply sporting a smile. It has to do with a fundamental internal stance.

Our Catholic spiritual and theological tradition can help. It reminds us unapologetically that definitions matter, and so it is with "joy." Saint Thomas Aquinas—the subject of a marvelous biography by Chesterton—has some helpful ideas here. He distinguishes between natural and spiritual joy. The interesting thing is that despite the differences, the two types of joy do share a common thread.

Natural joy, as Thomas describes it, is the emotion we experience when we are in the presence of a person we love, or simply when we know that a person whom we love is well. Sadness, then, is the opposite: when we are not with someone we love or we know they are suffering.

Spiritual joy relates this quality to God. It begins with an awareness of God's goodness and our consciousness of his loving presence in our lives. Saint Thomas takes it further by explaining that our spiritual joy comes from knowing that God is good, as well as participating in that goodness. We are joyful to the extent that we are consciously in communion with God, a communion rooted in prayer.

So now Saint Paul's exhortation makes sense. We can rejoice always because we trust that God—perfect goodness and love—is with us always.

Chesterton's reflection on the role of joy in the life of a Christian brings to mind both Paul and Thomas, and their words flesh out his. Reading him on joy gives us good insight into Chesterton as a pivotal player: it reveals his character as well as his always pertinent paradigm: some things are false, other things are true, and it doesn't make sense to align your own life with anything but the truth. And when you do this? Joy happens.

It comes down to this: the truth is that God exists, and that he created you and this world you live in. God is good and loving, and his creation is grace-filled and beautiful, and you are not separate from that, for God's loving graciousness is not an abstraction or an idea found in a book alongside other equally true ideas. It is the way it is—it is *true*.

Knowing the truth about how the world is and living that truth can, then, bring only joy. Under, through, and above all of the troubles and the stubborn, prideful sin, if we know the truth about the way things *really* are—sadness, as Chesterton says, is a blip. It's real, but it's small, and it doesn't govern our sense of the world or define our perspective.

All of us know the pain of loss—the threat to that natural joy of which Saint Thomas speaks. We've had to make decisions about how to go on. We make that decision in the wake not only of the loss of people to death, but all the other kinds of losses that almost literally pile up as we age: disappointment in others, disappointment in ourselves, disillusionment, concern about the way the world seems to be changing, a deeper awareness of how cruel and stupid human beings can be to one another.

In this regard, my life is not unique. I can't excuse myself from joy because Paul and Thomas were saints and they lived in simpler, less challenging times. For the fact is, they didn't. Saint Paul wrote as part of a minority persecuted by a powerful force in a corrupt and exploitive culture in which men, women, and children were enslaved and unwanted children were killed. Thomas lived in a challenging intellectual time and experienced great pain at the hands of his own family. Chesterton wrote *Orthodoxy* just a few years after the brutality of the Great War.

And they were all human beings: sinful, limited, suffering—and living, as is every one of us, in the shadow of death.

So where was their joy?

In truth. Not in feelings or responses to situations or a healthy self-image, but in the truth, above all, about who God is. All of our pivotal players return to this again and again, and are indeed grounded in the truth about God, not the vagaries of culture or opinions about what's important.

Chesterton reminds us that our decision for joy is rooted in the truth that God is, God loves, God reigns. It, like everything else in life, is based on the truth about life, something that is at the heart of all of Chesterton's writing: understanding the world correctly so we can understand how we fit, what make sense, and how God fits.

Often when we compare how a disciple should move through the world with the, well, worldly way of doing so, we focus on matters like wealth, material things, and sexuality. We also think in terms of measuring our external choices against precepts articulated in revelation and tradition. There's nothing wrong with that, but Chesterton challenges us to go even deeper and look to the root of it all. The world is a certain way. God is who God is. Is my fundamental stance expressive of worldly values or a trust in God?

In other words, quite simply, is praise the permanent pulsation of my soul?

<u>Consider:</u> *What is my fundamental stance regarding my daily life and my life and general? Does it reflect joy or something else? What holds me back from joy?*

<u>Pray:</u> *Loving God, you are the source of my life. Help me see the gift of this life, even in the face of difficulties and disappointment.*

G.K. CHESTERTON

SANITY AND REASON

For we must remember that the materialist philosophy (whether true or not) is certainly much more limiting than any religion.... Mr. McCabe thinks me a slave because I am not allowed to believe in determinism. I think Mr. McCabe a slave because he is not allowed to believe in fairies. But if we examine the two vetoes we shall see that his is really much more of a pure veto than mine. The Christian is quite free to believe that there is a considerable amount of settled order and inevitable development in the universe. But the materialist is not allowed to admit into his spotless machine the slightest speck of spiritualism or miracle.... But the materialist's world is quite simple and solid, just as the madman is quite sure he is sane. The materialist is sure that history has been simply and solely a chain of causation, just as the interesting person before mentioned is quite sure that he is simply and solely a chicken. Materialists and madmen never have doubts.

Spiritual doctrines do not actually limit the mind as do materialistic denials. Even if I believe in immortality I need not think about it. But if I disbelieve in immortality I must not think about it. In the first case the road is open and I can go as far as I like; in the second the road is shut.

G.K. Chesterton's manner of explaining the truth of Christianity is certainly unique. It is inductive, in a way, almost like the style of Saint Thomas Aquinas, beginning not with propositions or credal statements but with lived experience. Nature, if you will. Human nature.

Chesterton's journey was one of observing the world around him, noting its contradictions, conflicts, and deep themes. He also noted the ways that the world goes very, very wrong—ways in which, as he puts it, insanity takes hold.

When Chesterton speaks of "insanity" he obviously does not mean clinical mental illness, but rather a disengagement from reality. Psychoanalysis was a new, innovative field of study during Chesterton's life, and the vocabulary and paradigms it brought to the culture were all the rage. Chesterton, attuned to these cultural movements, was canny in his engagement with these popular concepts.

For Chesterton, a madman is not a person who has lost his reason, but rather someone who has lost everything but his reason and is tied into a narrow and all-explaining system, a system that by its nature is closed, one that admits only certain aspects of life and ignores what doesn't fit.

Chesterton is writing in the context of various movements and ideologies specific to his own time. In *Orthodoxy*, for example, he takes on various public figures and the ideologies of materialism and fatalism: the notions that the transcendent does not exist and that life is determined to proceed in a certain way because of economic or social factors.

The details of those ideologies and his arguments against them are perhaps not as relevant to contemporary readers as urgent modern problems, but the general point certainly is.

When we eliminate the transcendent and God-given human freedom from our perspective, what we end up with is an extremely confining and restrictive worldview. The materialist and the rationalist accuse the believer of being small-minded and narrow, but Chesterton likes to point out, as he does in the passage above, that the opposite is actually the case.

"Mysticism," he says later in *Orthodoxy*, "keeps men sane." Imagination, which could be described as a sort of mysticism, does as well. Both are more realistic than the self-proclaimed realism of the rationalist because both engage with the transcendent and admit to mystery. In admitting what cannot be explained or controlled, the believer, Chesterton says, actually understands much more than the rational materialist.

Chesterton was examining big ideas and movements, but it might be interesting to consider how this notion of mystery and materialism impacts our own lives in other ways. In other words, when I consider my own life, am I sane about it? Or am I mad, locked into that fixed system and chain of causation?

Consider life. Consider life—your life, my life, any of our lives. What are these lives? It is tempting, for example, to look at other people and think we know them—to judge them, even. How many categories do we casually and even unconsciously employ in our encounters as we move through the day? You're a cashier in the discount store, a mom in the private school car line, a kid loping down the street wearing baggy jeans, a guy with a gun rack in his pickup, a priest, an elderly man leaving Mass early, a woman in a hijab, an academic…white, black, Asian, African, Hispanic…don't tell me. Don't bother. I know who you are.

It's Chesterton's rationalist, writ smaller, right at home in my own head. How many times must I actually get to know a stranger before I learn how limiting my preconceived notions are?

All the same, Chesterton's sketch of the spiritual, intellectual, and imaginative freedom of the Christian is provocative, not only culturally, but personally. It's a challenge and an invitation. It's a challenge to take a good look at how I see my life. What defines it? My job? The walls of the room I'm sitting in? The parade of appointments and meetings that await me today? Is my relationship with all of this one of resigned acceptance of some sort of inevitable fate, or can I see deeper? It's not a matter of breaking free and changing what I do—although it well could be.

Materialism and rationalism of all sorts, even on a personal level, try to shape and define the world. It inevitably leaves things out. When we attempt to shape and define and limit, even our own lives, we miss things.

In my determination to get things done according to plan, what am I missing? In my judgment of others and my conviction that I understand them because of their social class, profession, or ethnicity, what am I missing? In my resigned conviction that I react to life in a certain way because of my family background or particular mental makeup, what am I missing? In my daily lived experience, running from one obligation to the next, focused only on the logistics and daily checklist, what am I missing?

As Chesterton points out, if all of this connects me to less rather than more, if it settles me in something less than the fullness of truth, how insane is that?

Consider: *In what ways am I a "rationalist" or "materialist" in my concept of myself? Of the world around me? Of the past and future of my own life? Of the lives of others?*

Pray: *Lord of heaven, open my heart, mind, and spirit to your presence through all of creation. Lift the limits of my sin, my biases, and my fears.*

G.K. CHESTERTON

THE ETHICS OF ELFLAND

I went over all the cases, and I found the key fitted so far. The fact that Swinburne was irritated at the unhappiness of Christians and yet more irritated at their happiness was easily explained. It was no longer a complication of diseases in Christianity, but a complication of diseases in Swinburne. The restraint of Christians saddened him simply because he was more hedonist than a healthy man should be. The faith of Christians angered him because he was more pessimist than a healthy man should be...

Paganism declared that virtue was in a balance; Christianity declared it was in a conflict: the collision of two passions apparently opposite. Of course they were not really inconsistent; but they were such that it was hard to hold simultaneously... And now I began to find that this duplex passion was the Christian key to ethics everywhere. Everywhere the creed made a moderation out of the still crash of two impetuous emotions.

Chesterton examined the world and human nature with an honest, perplexed eye. One of the keys to his conversion involved his working out the relationship between the world and what Christianity said about the world. Christianity expresses many apparent contradictions and, Chesterton thinks, is criticized roundly for it by those who say they value truth and consistency. But Christianity stubbornly holds to those apparent contradictions. Why doesn't it just give up and accept simple consistency? Why does it hold on to these opposites?

The critics of Christianity, Chesterton noted, focused on its purported vices, but it always seemed to be opposing vices. It was too pessimistic in its contempt for flesh, too optimistic in its promise of everlasting happiness. But how could both criticisms be valid? For, as Chesterton said, "Christianity could not at once be the black mask on a white world and also the white mask on a black world."

Did Christianity encourage its adherents to be too weak and timid to deal with reality, or was the promotion of the Crusades evidence of an inhumane, domineering tendency? Was it too monkish and austere or too accepting of worldly wealth and pomp?

What pervasive evil this Christianity must be, Chesterton observed—unless it wasn't:

> *Perhaps (in short) this extraordinary thing is really the ordinary thing; at least the normal thing, the center. Perhaps, after all, it is Christianity that is sane and all its critics that are mad, in various ways.*

Unless the truth was that, as Bishop Barron puts it, "perhaps Christianity was not so much oddly shaped as perfectly shaped, and perhaps those whose vision is distorted in various ways see it as, alternatively, too this and too that, just as various people might see one and the same man as too fat or too thin, too dark or too fair."

It is a startling and clarifying realization. The truth about the world is that both austerity and the rococo exist. The passionate, single-minded devotion to God of the celibate exists, as does the devotion to love God through a spouse and children. Life itself is woven of extremes and seemingly opposing passions.

Christianity, Chesterton concluded, reflects the truth of this life and this world. It does not, mind you, reconcile them into a balanced, diluted middle ground between extremes. There is nothing moderate about Christian heroes. Consider the rest of our pivotal players—Francis of Assisi, Catherine of Siena, Michelangelo, Thomas Aquinas, and Newman—as well as any of the other thousands of saints Catholicism celebrates. They're presented as models and intercessors. They are not living in a mushy middle of compromise between opposites. They are focused, passionate disciples of Jesus who, like the apostles, in answer to Jesus' invitation, drop their nets and go.

We see this radical and confident putting together of mutually exclusive extremes in the creed itself, where we boldly affirm that Jesus is not half-god and half-human. No, he is *fully* human and *fully* divine.

We also see it in the Christian understanding of the human person. As Chesterton observed, Christianity is taken to task for being both too pessimistic about human nature and too sunnily optimistic. Both, of course, are true. For at the heart of our faith and our understanding of ourselves is the very strange but real truth that human beings are capable of terrible things, and human achievements are quite properly criticized and honestly assessed in the ways they fall short and cause harm and destruction.

What's true of the human project writ large is also true of my own small, local human project called my life.

I have flaws, weaknesses, and a tendency to sin. I also am a creature beloved by God. My existence is not an accident. I'm here because God wants me to be, and he willed me—specifically me, this person right here—into existence. I am body and soul, flesh and spirit. The clash of opposites happens inside me every day.

What happens when I deny one or the other? When I forget my nature as a child of God and allow my weaknesses to lead the way? Or when I forget the goodness of which I am capable and which I am called to nurture, and think of myself, in despair, as stuck in the mire of my weaknesses?

And then what happens when I ignore my flaws and get caught up in that *imago Dei*? Bad things can happen then, as well. When I forget that the Christian understanding of deification happens mostly *after* death, not before, it's not only me that suffers the consequences.

Finally, what about others? Just as I want to be aware of my own proper end and the limitations I face in the journey, so I must be aware that every person I meet is built the same way. No other person is perfect, so I must be wary of the temptation to deify them or make idols of them or be too hard on people because they don't live up to an ideal. Nor, just as importantly, can I forget that the irritating people who drive me crazy or even shock or distress me are creatures made by God, loved by him, and being nudged towards him as well.

But then, here we are—weak, sinful human beings, who somehow are created in the image of God, are more like God than any other created thing, and have actually been created, as a matter of fact, for eternal communion with the Creator of the universe, with the ground of all existence.

Imagine that.

It doesn't make sense, the outsider says. Ah, says Chesterton, but maybe it does. Maybe it makes perfect sense, after all.

Consider: *What are the extremes in my life? What fundamental aspects of my personality do those extremes express? How can they be spiritually fruitful?*

Pray: *Jesus, you are the Word of God, through whom all was created; come among us as a child, as a man broken on a Cross. Help me to see your presence in life's paradoxes and mysteries.*

G.K. CHESTERTON

THE STRANGENESS OF MAN

Monkeys did not begin pictures and men finish them; Pithecanthropus did not draw a reindeer badly and Homo Sapiens draw it well. The higher animals did not draw better and better portraits; the dog did not paint better in his best period than in his early bad manner as a jackal; the wild horse was not an Impressionist and the race horse a Post-Impressionist. Other things may resemble it or resemble each other in various ways; other things may excel it or excel each other in various ways; just as in the furniture of a room a table may be round like a mirror or a cupboard may be larger than a mirror. But the mirror is the only thing that can contain them all. Man is the microcosm; man is the measure of all things; man is the image of God. These are the only real lessons to be learnt in the cave and it is time to leave it for the open road... The simplest truth about man is that he is a very strange being; almost in the sense of being a stranger on the earth.

Chesterton wrote *The Everlasting Man* as a response to H. G. Wells' book *Outline of History*. Wells had taken a view of history that was decidedly progressive, in the sense that he saw humanity as marching forward toward an ever-improving future, a progress in which religion was either irrelevant or a hindrance.

In response, Chesterton described history differently, with a more consistent core. Human beings, he posited, had always

123

been unique, and "progress" was not really the point of human history or existence.

So he begins his work with a chapter on "Man in the Cave." It was during the late nineteenth and early twentieth centuries that sensational discoveries of ancient cave paintings had been made in northern Spain and southern France. (Lascaux, the most well-known, would not be made until the 1940's, however, long after *The Everlasting Man* was written.)

Chesterton contemplates these paintings and wonders what they mean, concluding that they reveal, more than anything else, the distinctiveness of humanity. That uniqueness was already evident thousands of years ago—no "progress" required.

Human beings are significantly different from other creatures. We are the only creatures, Chesterton points out, who portray the nature around us. We are the only creatures who laugh, who feel shame, and, very importantly, we are the only creatures who know that we will die. As Bishop Barron says, "what the cave paintings reveal is that humans differ from other animals in kind and not merely in degree. Precisely as an artist, a creator, the human can mirror all other things, in some sense containing them all, and in this he is like God, the Creator of all... The human being has a *capax Dei*, a capacity for God. He is ordered to union with his Creator; or, in Biblical language, he is made in the image and likeness of God. And this is precisely what suits him to be open to the Incarnation, God becoming one of us."

One need not see these specific ancient works in order to appreciate Chesterton's point. Egyptian or pre-Columbian pyramids and calendars, the navigation techniques of Pacific Islanders, the intricate craftsmanship in every possible medium that ancient peoples have left behind, these all bear witness.

But reflecting on the past bears another type of witness. I may like to think that we fellow moderns are more sophisticated in another way as well: we, after all, know so much better. We are so much more tolerant and inclusive, less brutal and violent, more caring of all people and creatures.

But are we really? Perhaps we can reflect on the particular types of exclusion and violence that characterized ancient peoples and then take an honest look at our own time. Are we really so much more advanced?

Or, as Chesterton liked to point out, is the evidence for original sin any less powerful today than it was in ancient times?

Intriguingly, original sin, a Christian belief that some take as a criticism of humanity, is actually the opposite. As Chesterton says, to point out that humanity has fallen says quite clearly that we began somewhere higher than we are. We have fallen *from somewhere.*

Chesterton's description of the man in the cave also suggests another way to contemplate humility. I am unique as a human being, but it is not a uniqueness borne of my own power or even of the times I live in. I'm not unique because I can communicate instantly with people across the globe or because I live in a certain country, culture, and time period. Our uniqueness lies in who we are as created by God, not by what we have made ourselves to be. Humility is woven through with wonder. This humility links me to the man or woman in the cave.

Things have certainly changed. I can drive what would have been a day's journey in twenty minutes. I can wave at someone across the globe, I can look up at the moon and know that people have walked there.

But for what purpose? One can argue that yes, there is material "progress" of a sort, but what do I use it for? In the end, I—with my computer, my microwave, and my car—am no different than the person in the cave. We are both created by God in his image, with the capacity to create, to imagine, to reach, to love sacrificially.

We are, indeed, all rather strange—strange in that unique relationship to God, strange compared to the rest of creation. We dwell in mystery; we contemplate the mystery and are pulled by it; in any and every age, we pick up whatever instrument is at hand, and, seeking entry, we haltingly make a stroke.

Consider: *In what ways have we "progressed" in history? In what ways have we not? What binds us to peoples of the past?*

Pray: *Lord, in humility, I thank you for the gift of my creativity and the capacity to live in communion with you. May I live in deep and grateful awareness of this uniqueness.*

THE STRANGENESS OF CHRIST

What should we feel at the first whisper of a certain suggestion about a certain man? Certainly it is not for us to blame anybody who should find that first wild whisper merely impious and insane. On the contrary, stumbling on that rock of scandal is the first step. Stark staring incredulity is a far more loyal tribute to that truth than a modernist metaphysic that would make it out merely a matter of degree. It were better to rend our robes with a great cry against blasphemy, like Caiaphas in the judgment, or to lay hold of the man as a maniac possessed of devils like the kinsmen and the crowd, than to stand stupidly debating fine shades of pantheism in the presence of so catastrophic a claim. There is more of the wisdom that is one with surprise in any simple person full of the sensitiveness of simplicity, who should expect the grass to wither and the birds to drop dead out of the air when a strolling carpenter's apprentice said calmly and almost carelessly like one looking over his shoulder: "Before Abraham was, I am."

In the second part of *The Everlasting Man*, the strangeness of the Man in the Cave is graciously met by the even stranger God in the Cave.

And this is, Chesterton reminds us, a very, very strange thing.

Just as the first part of the book has an implied audience of evolutionists and devotees of progress, so does the second half: those who believe that Jesus, certainly an interesting and kind fellow and an intriguing teacher, is no more than that. He is just one of the great religious and moral teachers who taught something no more distinctive than Buddha or Mohammad, and is no more than a sign to the rest of us of the greatness humanity can achieve, and perhaps even the price that goodness sometimes has to pay at the hands of the powers that be.

But wait, says Chesterton. Really?

Begin with the whole premise of Jesus and how he came to walk among us. Despite the claims that the incarnation is simply repackaged Near Eastern mythology, of course, it is not. It is, as Bishop Barron says, something that begins with a "sublime jest.... The infinite and all-powerful God becomes a child born in a cave dug in the earth: the hands that made the sun and stars were too small to reach the huge heads of the cattle. Upon this paradox, we might almost say upon this jest, all the literature of our faith is founded. No other religion makes a claim anywhere near as radical and strange and wonderful as that."

The strangeness does not end there, of course. As Chesterton explores the figure of Jesus in the Gospels, he encounters strangeness at every turn. Jesus' teaching, when we look to what he actually says rather than the flattened out versions in our memories, is strong and radical, characterized by a sort of fierceness and even anger, tossing out impenetrable sayings— and then telling his disciples it's no accident.

Ultimately, though, what we must face are Jesus' claims about himself. As we read the Gospels, we hear it again and again, ways that his contemporary listeners heard quite clearly and were scandalized. First-century Palestine was no different than ours, in this sense. There was no lack of teachers, wise men, philosophers, or religious leaders. For the most part, they were left to sink or fall on their own.

But this Jesus?

He was crucified.

As Chesterton notes, the claims of Jesus, humbly and casually though they were articulated, are radical, unique, and strange. No religious or philosophical teacher had made claims quite like these, on their own behalf. The Chestertonian focus on the paradox begins here with God in a mother's arms, nursing from her breast, then decades later returned there, lying still in death. And in between, eying the synagogue crowd, announcing that prophecies were being fulfilled in their sight, forgiving sins, associating his own body with the Temple and his death with the covenant, his identity with the great *I AM*.

How in the world could this be? And how in the world does it become so ordinary, so unremarkable? How does the truth of Jesus, so clear from the Gospels, so startling, so challenging, so arresting, get tamed, flattened, drained, and modulated?

It can happen in many ways. Familiarity does it first, of course. In any relationship or element of our life, familiarity breeds, if not contempt, at least an unreflective acceptance. So it is with Jesus. If we are lifelong Christians, we have been hearing the Gospel narratives since we were small, have smiled as we have seen them acted out by children. We know how it went, we think; we assume we know how it goes, what it means, and how it ends.

We also tame Jesus by being selective, and this can happen in a couple of ways. First, even in our religious culture, Jesus can be cited selectively. Biblical scholars tell us what Jesus *really* did and did not say, which Jesus is the "authentic" Jesus, the real, historical Jesus.

But even in our own personal encounters, we can be selective. We tame Jesus by assuring ourselves that he didn't mean this, that saying doesn't apply to me, at least right now. We tell ourselves that Jesus lived in another time and place and was addressing his words to those people, not me.

We tame Jesus by bringing to bear all the typical sins: pride, mostly.

We tame Jesus by thinking he's talking to other people, not me, when he challenges.

We tame Jesus by convincing ourselves he's talking *only* to me, and not to every other person on earth, when he speaks of mercy, forgiveness, and the welcoming embrace of the Father.

We tame Jesus by not attending to the saints, who know him, listen to him, and change radically as a consequence.

Chesterton makes an argument, yes. But he also presents a challenge. In looking at the Gospel with fresh eyes, without taking anything for granted or assuming he knows it all already, he offers us a challenge, a strange one, even.

If Jesus is who he says he is, how can my life ever be the same?

Consider: *In what ways have I "tamed" Jesus? How do I diminish his radical call and even his divine claim on my life?*

Pray: *Jesus, Lord and Savior, may I be more attentive to your words, open to your presence, and willing to be surprised and changed by you.*

BL. JOHN HENRY NEWMAN

CONVERSION

Lead, kindly Light, amidst th'encircling gloom,
Lead thou me on!
The night is dark, and I am far from home,
Lead thou me on!
Keep thou my feet; I do not ask to see
The distant scene; one step enough for me.
I was not ever thus, nor prayed that thou
Shouldst lead me on;
I loved to choose and see my path; but now
Lead thou me on!
I loved the garish day, and, spite of fears,
Pride ruled my will. Remember not past years!
So long thy power hath blest me, sure it still
Will lead me on.
O'er moor and fen, o'er crag and torrent, till
The night is gone,
And with the morn those angel faces smile,
Which I have loved long since, and lost awhile!

Meantime, along the narrow rugged path,

Thyself hast trod,

Lead, Savior, lead me home in childlike faith,

Home to my God.

To rest forever after earthly strife

In the calm light of everlasting life.

The paths of converts are varied and complex. Moderns attempt to strip them down, looking for a powerful program that will grab the seeker's attention and bring her in the door. The line between evangelization and marketing can be a tricky one.

But when we actually examine the journeys of real converts, we are reminded that matters are not so simple. God reaches the human heart; the Spirit moves us in particular, peculiar, and surprising ways that can't be packaged, unless it's packaged in a big, messy, broad, and deep thing called the Catholic Church.

So it was with John Henry Newman. He was raised in the Anglican church—or the Church of England. Newman's family practiced a form of Anglicanism that leaned more towards a Protestant than a historical and sacramental emphasis—as did most Anglicanism of the time, which is important to Newman's story.

As Newman came to a deeper faith as an older adolescent, and then studied at Oxford University, he encountered a challenge to the more Protestant grounding of then-contemporary Anglicanism. He began reading the theological and spiritual writers of the early Church, who we called the Greek and Latin

Fathers, which then led him to a more "Catholic" perspective on faith.

Newman was already a Christian when he encountered these writers and then engaged with other similarly-minded young men at Oxford. But the way in which this involvement and his immersion in Christian history changed him is certainly a conversion of sorts.

It was a conversion that eventually, years down the road, led to a more formal conversion—to the Catholic Church. We think of it as inevitable, perhaps, but in the context of the time, it certainly was not. While the Oxford movement, as it was called, did indeed result in many conversions from Anglicanism to Catholicism, many also stayed in the Church of England. Nor were Newman's early encounters with the Catholic world indicative of his future move: in 1832, he visited Rome and was unimpressed with what he experienced as superstitious practices and accretions on the purer teachings of those early Church Fathers.

But eventually, Newman came to a realization. The question of doctrine, or Church teaching, absorbed him deeply. In his life as an Anglican he had attempted to strike a *via media* or "middle way" between Protestantism and Catholicism. As time went on, however, this struck him as untenable, a suspicion that was confirmed for him when he read Saint Augustine's adage *securus judicat orbis terrarium*, or "the whole world judges securely."

As Bishop Barron notes, what this revealed to Newman was that when it comes to determining truth, it is this Church that judges the truth of Christian doctrine: not the national, local church that was the Church of England or even the witness of four or five centuries of Patristic Fathers. It was the entire Church, across time and space. It had to be. And it had to be the one, universal, catholic—Catholic—Church.

Newman's way was long and fraught, even after his conversion. The journey was circuitous, impacted by various unexpected factors in unanticipated ways. Newman's understanding of this journey to the fullness of faith is summed up in the hymn above, *Lead, Kindly Light*. Newman wrote this as a poem in 1833, well before his 1845 conversion to Catholicism. He wrote it during the voyage to the continent that included his dissatisfying encounter with expressions of popular Catholicism in Rome, after having been forced to pause the journey for three weeks because of illness. So if we think of the ideal faith journey as a straight line from here to there with no ambiguities or questions, even this lovely, faith-filled poem sets us straight.

In it we see the qualities of Newman's mind and soul, condensed into a few lines, qualities that characterized his entire journey.

We see careful and honest self-assessment—I used to be confident and take pleasure in choosing my own way on my own terms. No more. Lead me on.

We see profound spiritual desire and openness to wherever God would take him, a dismantling of pride, and a willingness to turn from the "garish day" and endure whatever darkness was on the way to an authentic, profound communion with the Lord.

We see a confidence that no matter what the journey holds, that Light that leads is, above all, "kindly." God is love, and God lovingly guides us to him. It is his desire, and, in faith and hope, it is our desire as well.

No one journey of faith is identical with another. But all have some basic elements in common, elements that we can see in John Henry Newman's journey. No matter where I am on my particular path, whether I am searching, content, doubting, or confidently enthusiastic, I can be challenged by his example to examine my own path: am I dealing with God in complete honesty about myself? Or am I attempting to hide, or pretending to be who I imagine I should be, rather than who I actually am, flaws, sins, and all?

Am I on this path trusting in the Lord's goodness? Or do I harbor suspicions of God, or put God, ever so subtly, in opposition to me and my will?

Am I, in full trust, able to say to the Lord, as well, *Lead me on?*

Consider: *Am I willing to be led by God to an ever deeper relationship with him and his truth? Am I willing to pay whatever that might cost?*

Pray: *Lord, I trust in you, your light, and your love. You know me better than I know myself. Lead me on.*

BL. JOHN HENRY NEWMAN

The Price of Conversion

God has created me to do him some definite service. He has committed some work to me which he has not committed to another. I have my mission. I may never know it in this life, but I shall be told it in the next. I am a link in a chain, a bond of connection between persons.

He has not created me for naught. I shall do good; I shall do his work.

I shall be an angel of peace, a preacher of truth in my own place, while not intending it if I do but keep his commandments.

Therefore, I will trust him, whatever I am, I can never be thrown away. If I am in sickness, my sickness may serve him, in perplexity, my perplexity may serve him. If I am in sorrow, my sorrow may serve him. He does nothing in vain. He knows what he is about. He may take away my friends. He may throw me among strangers. He may make me feel desolate, make my spirits sink, hide my future from me. Still, he knows what he is about.

"Come," Jesus said. "Follow me."

And they did. The earliest disciples dropped their nets, left everything behind, and followed him. We don't know much about before, about what they sacrificed and left at the Lord's invitation. But we do know that they did this: they heard the voice of Jesus, and they allowed him to transform their lives completely and take them to a new, unanticipated place. Following Jesus took them to the Cross.

Then he said to them all, "If any want to become my followers, let them deny themselves and take up their cross daily and follow me." (Luke 9:23)

We see what this means in the lives of the saints, for they are actually ordinary people. We put them on pedestals (literally) and holy cards, but the truth is, we are all called to be saints, and, by cooperating with God's grace in profound ways, we can be.

Blessed John Henry Newman certainly denied himself and bore a cross. He was a well-known and highly respected Anglican clergyman, renowned for his preaching, when his intellect and conscience began to stir. The first indication of this shift was his involvement in the Oxford movement, a shift within Anglicanism that emphasized Catholic elements of the church, and one that stood apart from the mainstream of the more Protestant, even Puritan Anglicanism of the time.

When Newman wrote his "Tract 90", in which he argued that the "39 Articles"—the core statement of faith for the Church of England—could be given a "Catholic" reading, the reaction was swift. As Bishop Barron relates, Newman was condemned as a traitor "in every part of the country…through every organ and occasion of opinion, in newspapers, in periodicals, at meetings, in pulpits, at dinner tables, in coffee rooms, in railway carriages." In the wake of the controversy, Newman resigned his leadership of the Oxford movement and retreated into a time of intense study.

And at the end of this period, hardly knowing any Catholics at all, much less being part of any small Catholic community, Newman had come to understand the truth and his relationship to it. If the Catholic Church is the Church of Jesus Christ in a way that no other Christian body is, then that is where he must be.

Once a Catholic, he was, of course, reviled by his former co-religionists, but also, painfully, held as suspect by Catholics. He wrote to his sister:

> *I have a good name with many: I am deliberately sacrificing it. I have a bad name with more: I am fulfilling all their worst wishes, and giving them their most coveted triumph. I am distressing all I love, unsettling all I have instructed or aided. I am going to those whom I do not know, and of whom I expect very little. I am making myself an outcast, and that at my age—oh! what can it be but a stern necessity which causes this?*

And why go through all of this? As he wrote to fellow Tractarian John Keble, quite simply, "I consider the Roman Catholic Communion the Church of the Apostles."

This reaction to being seized by the Way, the Truth, and the Life that is Jesus Christ and that dwells in fullness in his Body, the Church, is not unique to John Henry Newman. We see it repeatedly and consistently in the saints. It is a characteristic of discipleship, in fact: saying "yes" to Christ means saying "yes" with one's entire life, and being willing to pay the price, to carry the cross, to deny whatever stands in the way.

What does saying "yes" in ever-deeper fullness and communion with the Lord mean for any of us?

Might it mean abandoning and saying "no" to certain aspects of life that are incompatible with the love, wisdom, and truth embodied in the Word of God? I might be called to deny myself small things that have become idols and that stand in the way of love. I might be called to make a huge change. Life in Christ might demand—yes, *demand*—that I definitively turn away from a particular activity or part of life. Jesus might also beckon me to say "yes" to something strange and new that is incompatible with the way things used to be.

Like John Henry Newman, we might experience a lack of understanding, or worse, from others. Many converts to faith in Jesus or even just deeper, more radical faith in Jesus find that, like Newman, they might be leaving a secure place for a place of risk and even loneliness. "O how forlorn and dreary has been my life ever since I have been a Catholic!" he wrote once.

This experience is certainly a challenge to us at any time, but perhaps even more so in times like these, when religion is often seen as a choice one makes in order to enhance one's quality of life. The saints reveal over and over that the peace one finds in Jesus Christ is not quite the same thing as "finding a church community that fits me and where I feel welcome."

John Henry Newman's journey situates us much differently. What is the appeal of faith in Jesus Christ to me? How deep, I must continually ask myself, does it really go? As Catherine of Siena wrote, even if we are sincere in our journey over Christ the bridge, our motives can remain selfish in the ways we seek to feed our emotional lives. Newman challenges me to look at my faith journey in a different light and to be open to an even deeper peace in the service of truth that lies at the end of a journey—a journey on strange, unfriendly, and sometimes even hostile roads.

Consider: *What has discouraged me in my faith journey? What has encouraged me?*

Pray: *Jesus, you are the Way, the Truth, and the Life. May I grow in faith and love and not be discouraged.*

BL. JOHN HENRY NEWMAN

THE DEVELOPMENT
OF DOCTRINE

It is indeed sometimes said that the stream is clearest near the spring. Whatever use may fairly be made of this image, it does not apply to the history of a philosophy or belief, which on the contrary is more equable, and purer, and stronger, when its bed has become deep, and broad, and full. It necessarily rises out of an existing state of things, and for a time savors of the soil. Its vital element needs disengaging from what is foreign and temporary, and is employed in efforts after freedom which become more vigorous and hopeful as its years increase. Its beginnings are no measure of its capabilities, nor of its scope. At first no one knows what it is, or what it is worth. It remains perhaps for a time quiescent; it tries, as it were, its limbs, and proves the ground under it, and feels its way. From time to time it makes essays which fail, and are in consequence abandoned. It seems in suspense which way to go; it wavers, and at length strikes out in one definite direction. In time it enters upon strange territory; points of controversy alter their bearing; parties rise around it; dangers and hopes appear in new relations; and old principles reappear under new forms. It changes with them in order to remain the same. In a higher world it is otherwise, but here below to live is to change, and to be perfect is to have changed often.

The life of Jesus spanned but thirty-three years, and the Gospels that tell his story are but four short books. What more do we need than that for faith? It seems pretty simple, doesn't it?

The question was asked by those at the heart of the Protestant Reformation, and John Henry Newman addressed it in his *Essay on the Development of Christian Doctrine*. Martin Luther and his followers had embraced *sola Scriptura* (Scripture alone) and rejected Catholic doctrine and structures as unwarranted additions to the core of apostolic faith.

In the *Essay*, Newman adds his own perspective to the age-old Catholic understanding of the role of tradition as legitimate, Spirit-guided developments of, not deviations from, the Gospel in the life of the Church.

As Bishop Barron says, "Newman argues that doctrines, like living organisms, evolve over time, gradually revealing the fullness of their meaning. This is because any idea is, as he puts it, 'commensurate with the sum total of its possible aspects.'" We can't know an idea fully until every dimension, face, and profile of that idea has disclosed itself, and that disclosure happens only over time. "There is no one aspect deep enough to exhaust the contents of a real idea."

In addition to time, this process requires the energy of a community of discourse. Ideas are mulled over, considered, compared, and contrasted to other ideas. They are all talked about, debated, tossed back and forth in lively argument—and in this way, they show forth their fullness. This development is not obscuring but clarifying.

As Newman concludes (in his ever-unfinished work), this process calls for a central, living voice of authority to discern the truth. Protestants would say this voice was the Bible itself, but the number of religious bodies, each resting their different truth claims on that Biblical authority, raises questions about that assertion. Only the Catholic Church had such a voice.

The temptation is strong—fueled by various currents in Christianity and in the world—to embrace the view that the purest Christianity is what is closest to the source, whether that be a "Bible only" approach or an emphasis on the historical words of Jesus stripped of the purported biases of the evangelists or a supposedly undiluted version of primitive Christian practice that includes Jesus, the apostles, and maybe Paul.

It's also a temptation that can arise even in the hearts of those committed to the Faith. Even if we recite the creed, are faithful in our religious duties, and are serious about our spiritual lives, we might just feel that, at times, we don't feel like going to Mass on Sunday morning. A Lent of fasting and abstaining, we're not at all looking forward to. A tough moral decision at work or in relationships, tough only because of the consequences I will have to bear as a result. The question of what to do with my material resources in a world of need.

And what do we feel in those moments? Excuses? Rationalization? Perhaps a voice that suggests that Jesus didn't really mean what he said, or perhaps didn't even say it at all? Or that since my issue isn't specifically addressed in the Gospels, I needn't worry about it? We re-open that old argument we might have had before with the whole of Catholic tradition, the one of spiritual practice, sacramental life, and mercy, in which we say "You're nice-looking and interesting, but I'll decide what I want to believe and do for now. Thanks."

It's the temptation to strip my faith of what makes me uncomfortable or inconveniences me, and, in the end, just like human beings have done since Adam and Eve, to set myself up as the ultimate judge of what's true.

As Newman points out to me in regard to these or any other spiritual issues, the central question is: *who decides?* It's about pride. It's about humility. It's about the starting point of my discernment.

If I begin with "what is the least I can believe?" then it's pretty certain that my winnowing will inevitably serve my own interests. It's just going to happen. We rarely decide that a teaching is closer to the "real" intentions of the early Christians or what I think Jesus "really" meant if it confounds our expectations or fails to serve our agenda. We see this again and again in Christian history. When aggressive pruning happens, it's usually at the service of an agenda. This is true when institutions and groups do the stripping, and it's true of us as well.

As John Henry Newman says so eloquently, time and the action of the Spirit have not weakened or diluted what God has revealed. On the contrary, I can trust that these waters are life-giving still, not in spite of the richness of the world in which God guides its flow, but precisely because of it.

Consider: *When am I tempted to set myself up as judge over the truth? What elements of the richness of my faith am I particularly grateful for?*

Pray: *Lord, thank you for the richness and depth of all that you have revealed. May I be open to receiving more, not less, open to being formed and nourished by your Word.*

BL. JOHN HENRY NEWMAN

THE IDEA
OF UNIVERSITY

[The Church] fears no knowledge, but she purifies all; she represses no element of our nature, but cultivates the whole. Science is grave, methodical, logical; with science then she argues, and opposes reason to reason. Literature does not argue, but declaims and insinuates; it is multiform and versatile: it persuades instead of convincing, it seduces, it carries captive; it appeals to the sense of honour, or to the imagination, or to the stimulus of curiosity; it makes its way by means of gaiety, satire, romance, the beautiful, the pleasurable.... Her principle is one and the same throughout: not to prohibit truth of any kind, but to see that no doctrines pass under the name of Truth but those which claim it rightfully.

We all have skills and areas of expertise and knowledge. We can cook, teach small children, lay electrical wire, argue a legal case, bind a wound, or manage a night shift. We are experts on ornithology, local history, human behavior, reptile behavior, economics, real estate, bluegrass, or maybe eighteenth-century Chinese literature. There are many specializations and strengths as human beings.

In *The Idea of the University*, a collection of lectures given in Dublin in 1852, John Henry Newman examines the issue of specialization— among many other topics, of course. He discusses the model of the research university composed of different specialized scholarly departments, common in our day, but a relatively new innovation from the continent in his. What role can religion have in this environment? How does theology fit in with study of mathematics, chemistry, history and literature?

Further, why study religion at all? In the late eighteenth and nineteenth centuries, academic theology was in flux, particularly in cultures rooted in Protestant Christianity. Theologians, Biblical scholars and religious movements were busy deconstructing Scripture as well as emphasizing the subjective and experiential dimensions of religions. Philosophy and theology had long since parted ways as disciplines. How could theology be an area for objective study in this context?

Newman, of course, argued strongly against these movements. Although the context of his lectures was specific to his time and place, many of the issues he addressed are still pertinent today, and so are his thoughts on them.

Whether we are particularly engaged with educational controversies or not, John Henry Newman's discussion of this question of specialization can still speak to us. For just as all of us are specialists in one way or another, so we can all succumb to the pitfalls of specialization that Newman describes.

For, as he puts it, it is all well and good and necessary to support particular areas of study and research. But if, as the educational leaders of his time would have it, theology were to be eliminated from that landscape, something important would be lost. A university, which by definition includes all disciplines, certainly ought to contain the discipline that speaks of God. In Bishop Barron's words, "religion ought to be, not only in the circle of disciplines, but at the center of it. In point of fact, the vacating of religion from the circle of university courses will lead, inexorably, to the supplanting of religion by some other discipline. This will take place because of a deep human instinct toward the philosophic, by which Newman means a passion for the whole, for a totalizing vision."

And this will result in a skewing of every discipline. For example, if one of the physical sciences takes the central place, if we begin to see all reality through a scientific lens, we will distort or altogether miss huge swaths of reality. Similarly, if everything is read from the standpoint of economics—as it is, for instance, in all forms of Marxism—then the arts, philosophy, and culture are appreciated as but epiphenomena of an economic substructure. The permanent expulsion of religion from the university would result, Newman predicted, in a constant succession of false pretenders to centrality.

So it is with me and my specializations and particular ways of interpreting world. I'm a limited human being, not an omniscient God, so of course I have angles and particular perspectives through which to interpret the world, but what happens when that mode of interpretation becomes not a clarifying window but a set of blinders? I've done it—when I can't put away the teacher hat and end up giving lectures to anyone in the vicinity. Or when the parent glasses won't allow me to see an adult child as, well, an adult. Confident in my own perspective, even unconsciously so, my empathy weakens, my pride increases, and, in the end, I know less rather than more.

In one of the lectures, Newman speaks of the specialist who lets his confidence in one area spill over into areas about which he knows considerably less: "You might think this ought to make such a person modest in his enunciations; not so: too often it happens that, in proportion to the narrowness of his knowledge, is, not his distrust of it, but the deep hold it has upon him, his absolute conviction of his own conclusions, and his positiveness in maintaining them. He has the obstinacy of the bigot, whom he scorns, without the bigot's apology, that he has been taught, as he thinks, his doctrine is from heaven."

Theology, Newman says, is not a lens that sits alongside other lenses. It is the fullest lens that offers the wearer the most accurate, holistic vision of reality. As he says in the passage above, the Church cultivates the whole, because it reflects, not the concerns of any smaller element, but the concerns of God.

So it is with my own vision. I can, it is true, only see what I can see with my limited perspective, experiences, and interests. But faith in my own life functions as Newman says that theology functions in the life of the university. I know that my own understanding is narrow and that there is, in fact, a greater, fuller understanding that belongs to God alone. Living with this awareness, I cannot help but value humility, empathy, and openness, for I know that, by myself, I can hardly see anything at all.

Consider: *What are my particular areas of interest and specialization? How do they enhance my vision and experience? How do they limit it?*

Pray: *Lord of light, expand my vision. Help me see the world humbly, with the open, clear eyes of faith.*

BL. JOHN HENRY NEWMAN

THE GRAMMAR
OF ASSENT

The heart is commonly reached, not through the reason, but through the imagination, by means of direct impressions, by the testimony of facts and events, by history, by description. Persons influence us, voices melt us, looks subdue us, deeds inflame us. Many a man will live and die upon a dogma: no man will be a martyr for a conclusion. A conclusion is but an opinion; it is not a thing which is, but which we are "quite sure about"; and it has often been observed, that we never say we are sure and certain without implying that we doubt. To say that a thing must be, is to admit that it may not be. No one, I say, will die for his own calculations: he dies for realities. This is why a literary religion is so little to be depended upon; it looks well in fair weather; but its doctrines are opinions, and, when called to suffer for them, it slips them between its folios, or burns them at its hearth.

Credo. I believe.

But what? What do we believe, and what do we even mean by belief and faith?

Jesus begins his public ministry with the call to faith: "Repent, and believe in the good news" (Mark 1:14). He asks his apostles as they tremble during a storm, "Why are you afraid, you of little faith?" (Matt 8:26). He tells the woman who had been hemorrhaging for years that her faith had saved her. And after his Resurrection he said to Thomas, "Have you believed because you have seen me? Blessed are those who have not seen and yet have come to believe" (John 20:29).

Having faith is complex and dynamic. We can experience certitude in a flash: knowing without doubt that we are loved by God, that Christ is truly present in the Eucharist, that the Risen Christ is real and means what he says about eternal life. We hear the voice of Christ, we sense his presence, we see storms calmed, and we *know*.

It is also possible to believe in a religious teaching with our intellect without feeling much intensity about it—or, conversely, knowing the truth of a tenet of faith from the depths of the heart without being able to really articulate or explain it. And sometimes, the deep and sincere hope that something really is true is as close as we can get.

John Henry Newman was, not surprisingly, fascinated by the question of faith, particularly faith and reason. His last great work, *The Grammar of Assent*, explored the topic, particularly the question of how we come to faith, what moves us to say, "I believe this is true."

A central issue, as anyone who engages in discussions on apologetics knows, is the question of evidence. In our day, as in Newman's, the truth of a proposition is as strong as the evidence given to support it. Can you *prove* that God exists or that Jesus really rose from the dead or that the Bible is the Word of God? Well, if you can't provide enough good evidence, those propositions must therefore be untrue, the argument often goes.

What Newman did was to turn the question a bit by rejecting the assumption that certitude based on evidence is the root of religious faith. Instead, he talked about "assent"—the psychological and intellectual act of accepting a proposition—and then two types of assent: notional and real.

Notional assent is the acceptance of "notions" or ideas. In real assent, we come to accept "concrete things, images, and impressions." It is the difference, as Bishop Barron points out, between accepting the immorality of slavery in principle and then being moved, by real examples, to a deep acceptance of its evil, an acceptance that moves one to action.

In the passage above, Newman vividly describes the difference. The distinction—one whose assent is real and not simply notional, will accept martyrdom. We die, as he says, for realities, not conclusions.

This difference is also made known in the conscience, the ground of real assent. Newman points out that conscience is characterized as a "voice"—an acknowledgment of relation and personhood that we don't apply to ideas or conclusions with which we agree in general. As Bishop Barron points out, "Somehow we know through conscience that we have pleased or offended a person by our actions, indeed a person powerful enough to see all of our acts and to press upon us unconditionally."

This is not to disparage the role of propositions and formulations of faith. The concept of real assent actually works to strengthen their importance, as it makes clear that the words are rooted in the Word of God. Knowing this, we pause for a moment before we begin the Nicene Creed at Mass or the Apostles' Creed at the start of our Rosary, and we open both our minds and our hearts to the truth—one truth expressed in words, ideas, and the vivid, real image before us of Christ crucified. We stand with the centurion then, and we hear, "Truly, this man was the Son of God."

The mutual interaction between notional and real assent evokes another sort of response as well. As Newman indicates in the passage above, real assent moves us to action. Saying yes to a reality—to the reality of the loving God who created and redeems us and the entire world—we say yes to all God says yes to. And we go forth; we can't help it.

Pope Benedict XVI was deeply influenced by the thought of John Henry Newman. At a prayer vigil the night before he beatified Newman in 2010, he drew the connections between these various types of assent and the evangelizing dynamic of real assent to the truth that is Jesus Christ:

Finally, Newman teaches us that if we have accepted the truth of Christ and committed our lives to him, there can be no separation between what we believe and the way we live our lives. Our every thought, word, and action must be directed to the glory of God and the spread of his Kingdom. Newman understood this, and was the great champion of the prophetic office of the Christian laity. He saw clearly that we do not so much accept the truth in a purely intellectual act as embrace it in a spiritual dynamic that penetrates to the core of our being. Truth is passed on not merely by formal teaching, important as that is, but also by the witness of lives lived in integrity, fidelity and holiness.

Consider: *What aspects of notional and real assent do I discern in my own life? At this moment, what aspects of my faith draw my deepest assent?*

Pray: *Along with the father of a child healed by you, Lord Jesus, I pray, "I believe, Lord. Help my unbelief!"*